Intimacy

Intimacy

A Green Light for Red Hot Sex and a Lifetime of Loving

JEFFRE TALLTREES, PH.D.

ORV. FRY, M.A., M.F.T.

Blue Dolphin Publishing

Copyright © 2001 Jeffre TallTrees and Orv. Fry
All rights reserved.

Published by Blue Dolphin Publishing, Inc.
P.O. Box 8, Nevada City, CA 95959
Orders: 1-800-643-0765
Web: www.bluedolphinpublishing.com

ISBN: 1-57733-056-0

Library of Congress Cataloging-in-Publication Data

Talltrees, Jeffre.
   Intimacy : a green light for red hot sex and a lifetime of loving / Jeffre Talltrees, Orv. Fry.
     p. cm.
   ISBN 1-57733-056-0
    1. Sex. 2. Sex in marriage. 3. Intimacy (Psychology) I. Fry, Orv. II. Title.

HQ21 .T14 2000
306.7—dc21

00-029243

Front Cover Painting "Ecstasy"
ART FOR COLLECTION, No. 1 in the fourth series of 8 paintings
and poem, "Ecstasy" on page v
by Catherine Andrews
© Copyright MCMLXXV Catherine Andrews, All Rights Reserved
For Website information on more paintings and their reproduction
as cards and prints and for music and CD
go to www.skylight.cc or www.catherineandrews.com

Printed in the United States of America

10 9 8 7 6 5 4 3 2 1

ECSTASY

Spiraling up out of the Vortex
then rushing to open
into the Higher Astral. This so lightened with color . . .

it will sun you in the warmth that springs Eternally.

You drink of my nectar
I drink of yours.
We lose all sense of difference
with Nothing, between us.
Blending soft and delicious
Your body is my body
Your heart is my heart
My life and soul is yours
And yours is mine
forever
In this sharing of Love.

                                        Catherine Andrews
                                        cover artist

Table of Contents

Foreword	viii
Introduction	x
Section 1: The Foundation for a Great Relationship	**1**
1. Sex and Sexual Beliefs: What Is Sex and What Are My Beliefs	3
2. Attitudes that Promote Personal Growth	11
3. Communicating for Greater Intimacy	20
4. Rescue in Relationship or How to Ruin a Good Relationship Fast	36
5. Emotional Intimacy for Going Deeper	43
6. Emotional Support and Stroking	51
7. Passion in Everyday Life	57
8. Balancing Our Lives for Health and Joy	65
9. Self-Esteem and Body Image	72

Section 2: Sex, Love and You — 79

10. Gender Differences: Yes, Virginia, Men and Women Come from Different Planets — 81
11. Anger and Sex Make Terrible Bed Partners — 88
12. Love and Affection — 96
13. Romance to Warm Up Your Nights and Days — 101
14. Health and Hygiene — 110
15. Good Sex Is Letting Go — 114
16. Touch to Enhance Your Life — 120
17. Self-Pleasuring Is for Grown-Ups — 128
18. Advanced Pleasuring When You're Ready — 137
19. Giving Yourself Permission to Be Fully Sexual — 147
20. Thinking Passionately: You Are What You Think — 153
21. Arousal and Desire: It's More Than Biology — 159
22. Loveplay, Every Day in Every Way — 165
23. Keeping It Playful for Eternal Loving — 172
24. Spirituality and Sex — 181
25. Putting It All Together for Sexual Ecstasy for a Lifetime — 187

Appendix — 203
    Reading List — 203
    Sexual Dysfunction — 207
    Safer Sex, Smart Sex — 212
    Information for Therapists Using This Playbook — 214

Index — 215

Foreword

Welcome to the world of the inquiring mind. Just by picking up this book you have opened a door into a realm that beckons to the brave heart. Come in. Linger a while, and explore the inner and outer spaces of Love, Intimacy and Sexuality with your guides, Jeffre TallTrees and Orv Fry by your side.

It takes powerful, insightful people like Orv and Jeffre to take you through the tangled underbrush of ignorance, fear and misinformation surrounding these topics. Where did you learn anything about sexuality or intimacy? Who were your teachers? Where did they learn what they have passed on to you, and what have you done with their teachings? See why it takes a brave heart to explore this realm? You are a pioneer on the frontier of yourself. This book will definitely assist you in having a better life for yourself and any others you may choose to have a relationship with.

However, what I have discovered in more than three decades working with people in the field of Love, Intimacy and Sexuality is that we long for it, but "it" eludes us. The "it" is everything that makes us delicious human beings. Such as Love. What is it? Where do I get it? Am I lovable? What do I need to do to make you love me? What does love look and feel like? And so much more.

When we talk about Sex and Intimacy we are virtually like the three blind men at the hind end of an elephant, attempting to figure out what the rest "looks like." The average human body is 3500 square inches of skin. Where is sex in those thousands of square inches? We haven't even included the mind, heart and soul. How big are they? Where do they exist, or do they? Many people say their heart and soul have never been touched in sex. And when we talk about intimacy, it appears that most people hunger for it, but again—what is it, really, and where do you get it? It sure doesn't appear to be readily available during sex, as most people practice it. Many people describe sex like the styrofoam container most fast-food meals come in, rather than a sumptuous banquet where you linger and enjoy to your heart's content.

Well, it's obvious that you got this book because you were interested in having the banquet. So, make yourself as comfortable as you can, and start digesting this wonderful banquet that "chefs" Jeffre and Orv have served up for you. Bon appétit!

>	Stan Dale
>	Doctor of Human Sexuality and
>	Founder, Human Awareness Institute

Introduction

When the fire of lust in a relationship has died, there is little fuel available to spark hot, loving sex. We believe the fuel for an enduring, passionate, love affair is the ever growing depth of intimacy reached by a couple.

We have drawn this conclusion after 50+ years of clinical experience where we have consistently seen individuals with sexual issues who have limited intimacy skills and abilities.

WHAT IS INTIMACY?

Intimacy is that interchange and feeling created when two humans have the courage to truly be their real selves with one another. Sharing on an intimate level with your partner means fully revealing parts of your physical, emotional and spiritual self as you evolve and grow. We call it telling your truth, or being honest.

The essence of intimacy is feeling open, real and accepted. This creates a charged, dynamic symbol of that intimacy found in sexual union. When there is intimacy, there is a comfort level created to support great sex. There is a trust of not being judged, a knowing that your true sexual self can feel joy and be enjoyed by your partner's true sexual self, thus creating a circular flow of sexual pleasure and deepening intimacy.

This entire "playbook" is about the relationship of intimacy, love and sex, about the interplay of physical and emotional intimacy. We believe that, ultimately, there is no separation between physical and emotional intimacy. These are united within each human being. Humans express their love and playfulness through sex because we are very sexual beings. Our sexuality is at the root of who we are, literally and figuratively.

Humans are very complex, broad and deep. Because there are only so many sexual positions, sexual boredom can take over in a long-term relationship. However, when intimacy is the basis for a loving relationship, the depth and possibilities for sexual exploration become infinite. The couple is no longer bound to the known. Life, love and sex become an endless journey of delight and discovery. Intimacy is the juice that keeps the relationship alive, vital, and ever new.

When intimacy is the basis for a loving relationship, the depth and possibilities for sexual exploration become infinite.

Our hope is that reading this book will give you the vision and the tools to create a complete sexual and loving intimate relationship. Using these tools will not only add to the quality of your relationship, but to your individual life as well.

Although there may not be consensus in the general population as to the nature of healthy sexuality, we have written this playbook to allow you to examine your belief systems and patterns of behavior so you, the reader, can explore and open yourself and your sexuality to a vast and ever evolving way of being with your partner. Let go of the concept of "normal" and simply enjoy the journey.

In Chapter 26, we describe what we believe a healthy sexual person to be. In the same chapter we list the 13 keys for sexual ecstasy and ongoing intimacy in a long-term relationship. Yes, this could be called super sex, but it is within the reach of any couple willing to give it some attention. Healthy sex is sexuality that keeps expanding, while defying common definitions and measures. **Great sex is a totality: a circle of love, tenderness, caring, spirit, playfulness, connection, exploration, and adventure** while being a fundamental source of emotional strength and health for the individual and the couple.

We, Orv. and Jeffre, are not sitting as objective observers, but as real life people involved in relationship. We continue to grow and evolve using these practices and developing skills to deepen and enrich our own marriages. We experience juice, excitement, health, passion and an overall turned-on quality of life. We see our lives and our relationships as a living laboratory in which these skills have been and will continue to be honed.

ABOUT THIS PLAYBOOK

This "playbook" has been written for the individual or couple who has chosen to look at him/her self and desires to have deeper intimacy and better sex in their relationship. Although this playbook is oriented for heterosexual couples, same sex couples will find it very useful as well. References will be in a heterosexual context, but we have found relationship issues to be very similar regardless of sexual preference.

We have chosen to call this a "manual" rather than a workbook for multiple reasons. A manual implies hands-on, of which there will be much as you move through the practices. We are not calling it a workbook because we believe that the primary joy of sex is the actual fun and play of sex. Sometimes we will call this book a manual and sometimes a playbook.

Do you and your partner need a playbook about sex? Who needs a playbook on sex? With more than fifty combined years of clinical experience, the authors believe anyone or any couple can benefit and make their sexual relationship even better.

This manual is written primarily for the committed heterosexual couple who has a reasonably good relationship. We do not intend for it to be a substitute for competent counseling. We are assuming that you can talk to each other about feelings and important personal issues.

Perhaps you can recall that your sexual relationship used to be hotter. Maybe you have always wanted to make changes in your sexual relationship. Perhaps you and your partner sincerely want to put more sizzle in your sexual life. Regardless of your personal reasons for choosing to follow this program, it is important for those who are experiencing serious sexual dysfunction, such as erectile problems, inorgasmia, pre-ejaculation, etc., to consult a qualified sexual specialist.

When you have completed this playbook, you will have many tools to promote the ongoing evolution of your sexual relationship as well as your complete relationship. We believe strongly that the quality of one's sexual relationship is directly related to the depth of intimacy experienced in the overall relationship.

FORMAT

Each chapter is a different topic. We have carefully designed this playbook so that optimal results will be obtained if read and practiced in the order presented. If for some reason you do not like the order or wish to skip around, each chapter stands on its own. Be sure you and your partner have a mutual agreement to do that. Try to complete each chapter. You will get more out of it.

Each chapter will take about two to four hours to complete. We hope you will want to do the entire chapter at one time. Each chapter includes information as well as practices to speed your learning. Doing the practices completely and in order will dramatically increase the benefits you receive. However, it is always better to do some rather than do nothing. (We don't give bad marks if you don't follow the instructions.) In each chapter we introduce real people and actual couple situations to remind you that you are not alone and are not the first to have a challenge in your love life.

MAKING TIME: THE FIRST STEP

For any long-term relationship to be successful, each partner must give it top priority in their life. In other words, **your relationship must come first—before friends, family and work.** This may sound bold or weird, but remember the intimacy and eagerness you both felt when courting. Recall the amount of time you spent thinking about your partner, not to mention the time the two of you actually spent together. By giving your relationship greater time and attention, you can recapture much of the excitement and passion you once felt for one another. It truly can be as simple as that.

The authors recommend that the couple read the text of the chapter together, perhaps taking turns reading it out loud. Be sure to stop and talk about points that you particularly think are important, that you want to add to, or that you have questions about. The practices are self-explanatory. You can decide together how you want to do it. Try to follow the outline as closely as possible.

Section 1

The Foundation for a Great Relationship

1

Sex and Sexual Beliefs: What Is Sex and What Are My Beliefs

WHAT IS SEX?

> Her hand closed around an enormous, blood-gorged pole of muscle. It pulsated in her hand like an animal and almost weeping with grateful ecstasy she pointed it into her own wet, turgid flesh. The thrust of its entering, the unbelievable pleasure made her gasp . . . and then like a quiver, her body received the savage arrows of his lightning-like thrusts . . . arching her pelvis higher and higher until for the first time in her life she reached a shattering climax. . . .
>
> from *The Godfather* by Mario Puzo

We have all been exposed to these mental images and sexual fantasies. The man who is erect and always ready. The woman who needs just the right man to fulfill her sexual dreams and awaken her sleeping eroticism.

Is this sex? Well, yes, and no! Yes, it is a limited window into the wide world of sex and sexuality. However, it is a very constricted view which perpetuates myths, expectations, and feelings of inadequacy for both men and women.

SEX AND SEXUALITY

Sex *can be* a powerful psychological, biological, socio-cultural and philosophical experience. Sex begins for most couples with passion and as a can't-wait-to-be-with-you experience. Sadly, for many it slowly evolves into a mundane, boring experience

"Sex" is often used to mean the physical act of intercourse. We feel very strongly that sex and sexuality has a much broader meaning. Sexuality is an aspect of one's self and one's lifestyle, much more than just something that one does. How you feel about sex and your own sexuality profoundly affects your perception, your sensations, and, literally, your experience.

Sexuality is an aspect of one's self and one's lifestyle.

When you think of the word, "sex," what pictures come to your mind? Do you think of the man on top? How about kissing on a subway? What about taking your clothes off slowly and sensually for no one except yourself? Many different factors influence the images that come to mind. Your age is very important. If you are over 60, it is quite likely you think about sex pretty traditionally. The younger you are, the more likely you have had intercourse at a younger age and experimented with various partners. Where you grew up will also affect your images and expectations. Your ethnic and religious background can also have profound effects on what you think and feel about sex.

It is our personal and professional goal to help people understand that **sex is so much more than intercourse.** It is an essential part of the fabric of your life.

Our English language is limited when it comes to descriptive words about sex and sexual behaviors. We want you to think of sex as an integral part of your being. After all, you exist because of a sexual act. Sex is what you think, feel, and do that feels pleasurable to the senses in a particular way you have come to define as sexual. Because **you** have defined it, you can continue to redefine it, indefinitely. *Sex is what you think it is* and more! Sex may be playful. It may be erotic. It may be angry or tender. There is no one right way to be sexual. There are multiple and ever evolving ways of being sexual, even when you choose to have the same sexual partner for the rest of your life. Ultimately, your definition of sex or sexuality is limited only by your imagination and willingness to explore. If you are in a partnership, it is important that both partners agree as to the direction and content of your exploration. Needless to say, this emphasizes the need for good communication skills. (Please refer to Chapter 3, Communication for Intimacy.)

Ultimately, your definition of sex or sexuality is limited only by your imagination and willingness to explore.

We are all sexual beings and almost anything can be considered sexual if it excites us, is consensual and not destructive. The more we narrow our definition of sex, the quicker sex will become boring and dissatisfying. A good, healthy sex life is enhanced by the ability to be playful, curious, open, and risking. Being sexual is as much a part of being human as breathing, eating, and exercising.

Remember, there is no "Right" definition for sex. It is as unique as the individuals who are defining it. With open, honest and complete communication with your partner, you will be able to arrive at new depths of joy and pleasure that will feel comfortable to you as a couple.

SEXUAL BELIEFS AND BEHAVIORS

We live in a society that gives two conflicting messages about sex. Nudity and sexuality are blatantly displayed on national media while the covert message continues to be that sex is evil, sinful, and dirty. Little girls and boys grow up with these confusing messages. Most adults are ambivalent and uncomfortable with the subject of sex. Our school's sex education courses are often sterile and academic without meaningful discussions of feelings, sensations, or pleasure. No wonder most of us are confused by the time we get married. Where are we supposed to learn "how to."

The United States of America, as well as most other Western societies, are anti-pleasure and anti-ecstatic. Since sexuality is an important element and source of pleasure and ecstasy, it makes sense that the beliefs we hold will reflect these values.

Although young women and men are having more sexual experiences at younger ages, ignorance is pervasive. Most men and women, when questioned privately, admit their first sexual experience was anxiety provoking and unsatisfactory, often resulting in more questions than answers.

Religious teachings are frequently the source of much confusion, guilt, and shame. Because human sexuality varies dramatically by culture and sect, each individual has to answer personal questions about his or her beliefs regarding the purpose and nature of sex and sexuality.

Sexuality is a natural part of being human. It can be very pleasurable and rewarding on many levels. When coupled with love and affection, sexuality can touch deep levels of enjoyment, intimacy, ecstasy, fulfillment, and spirituality.

· · · · ·

When Suzanne and Craig came in for their first appointment, Suzanne complained that Craig only seemed to be interested in achieving orgasm. He felt angry if she did not orgasm, although he frequently came quickly. Foreplay was cursory at best. Both admitted it was really hard to talk about sex without getting defensive. Both Suzanne and Craig had great justifications to explain why it was the other person's fault. Using the Sexual Beliefs and Behaviors practiced in this chapter, Suzanne and Craig explored their beliefs about sex. Both concluded that much of the challenge was not knowing what to talk about. They weren't certain that talking about sex was okay. Craig felt bad that he didn't know "it all" and did not want to hear Suzanne's complaints, however loving her intent, because it meant he was inadequate. So, understanding your own sexual beliefs is a good place to start. Communicating them to your partner is a terrific second step.

Craig discovered that as a young person he had received virtually no information about sex and mutuality in a sexual relationship. He thought it was all up to him, including Suzanne's orgasms. Suzanne learned that she carried much embarrassment and shame about sex from her early religious teachings and had not believed that she was supposed to talk openly about sex or flaunt her sexuality. Both Craig and Suzanne believed the myth that the man was primarily responsible for a couple's sexual relationship. After this exercise, it was much easier for them to open up communication and ask for what each wanted. The practice gave them more confidence that there are real answers to their questions.

Practice

SEXUAL BELIEFS AND BEHAVIORS

Purpose: To facilitate awareness of you and your partner's sexual attitudes, experiences and preferences.

- **You will each need a sheet of paper and a pen in preparation for this practice. Do your lists separately and then come together to discuss.**
- **Give yourself adequate time to give careful consideration to each item.**
- **Including discussion, this practice may take one hour or more.**

1. List all verbal and non-verbal messages you received from your mom about sex. (No message is a message.)
2. List all verbal and non-verbal messages you received from your dad about sex.

3. How do you think your mom felt about sex? What about her early life and family of origin that led to her feeling and believing as she did?

4. How do you think your dad felt about sex? What about his early life and family of origin that led to his feeling and believing as he did?

5. What messages did you get about sex from others (siblings, friends, etc.) when you were growing up? And in what way? i.e. magazines, verbally, movies, etc.

6. What and when was your first sexual experience?

7. When did you first have sexual intercourse? How was that experience for you?

8. Have you ever had a same sex experience? How did you feel about it then? How do you feel now?

9. Describe the most exciting and satisfying sexual experience you've had.

10. Describe the sexual fantasy that you find most erotic.

11. How do you feel about fantasizing about another person while being sexual with your partner?

12. What is the area of your sex life you'd most like to improve and change?

13. What is the area of your sexual life that you feel most satisfied with?

14. How frequently do you talk to your partner about sex? How comfortable do you feel talking to your partner about sex?

15. What percentage of time are you able to totally let go sexually, i.e., not be in your mind?

16. What percentage of the time do you feel under pressure or anxious about your performance? That of your partner?

17. What percentage of time do you have sex when you really don't want to?
18. Have you ever faked an orgasm? Why did you fake it?
19. What do you most enjoy about your sex life?
20. What would you like more of in your sex life?
21. Do you ever use sex to manipulate or power-play your partner?
22. What sexual thoughts, feelings or behaviors do you have that cause you to feel shame or embarrassment?
23. What sexual thoughts, feelings or behaviors does your partner have that causes you to feel shame, embarrassment or disgust? (You may choose to share these with your partner in writing first and talk about it later.)

- **You are encouraged to share your responses with your partner.**
- **Make an agreement with your partner to set aside time to *really* listen to each other's responses.**
- *Please listen only for understanding.*
- **Be sure to be *non-judgmental.***
- **If feelings should come up while doing this practice, set aside a separate time with your partner to discuss the feelings, and keep the appointment you make!**
- **For more suggestions about communication, see Chapter 3. You may want to play your way through Chapter 3 and then return to your discussion of sexual beliefs while working together on this practice.**

There is no right or wrong way to respond to these questions. As you move through the playbook, you will understand the meaning more and more. This is the first practice. As we have intended, each practice is designed to help you get to know *you* better.

• • • • •

This was the second marriage for both Sally and Bill. Although sex had been hot during courtship, both realized—after this exercise about beliefs—that verbal communication about sex had been noticeably absent from their relationship.

Sally was very surprised to learn that Bill sometimes faked orgasms. Bill was amazed to find out that Sally really liked oral sex, both fellatio and cunnilingus. She had just gone along and expected Bill to suggest it or try it. But because his previous wife did not like oral sex at all, he assumed that Sally did not either.

• • • • •

Arguments were a big part of Mary and Joe's six-year marriage. Arguments often ended with Mary screaming and Joe withdrawing both emotionally and physically. Each admitted feeling frustrated, powerless, and hopeless when they came for their first appointment.

During this initial practice, it became obvious to both Joe and Mary that they were trying to judge or control much of the other's behavior or feelings. It helped when they could see the controlling behavior, but they really made progress when they began to listen for understanding and tried to accept each other's feelings and beliefs. Needless to say, this is not a simple task when both partners tend to be blamers, but this exercise seemed to create a new awareness of their behavior.

• • • • •

We'll be checking in periodically with these couples to find out how they have used this playbook to enhance their relationship and their sexual lives.

2

Attitudes that Promote Personal Growth

Attitudes are mind sets which reflect deep-seated beliefs about yourself, others and relationships. Many of these beliefs are deeply rooted in our early childhood experiences and perceptions.

Perhaps you learned to listen in a non-judgmental way because that was the way your mother listened to you. In contrast, if you grew up in a family where either or both of your parents were very critical of you, as well as of each other, you probably grew up as a critical, blaming adult. Since this picture is usually coupled with an adult who was not listened to as child, chances are you could benefit with some listening practice. Fortunately, most of us grew up with a little bit of everything. We may be more critical than we need to be, and we probably could use some additional listening skills.

A non-judgmental attitude relates to yourself as well as to others. It is an attitude which facilitates any communication process. It is a recognition that people do what they do because it is who they are. Most people do the best job they know how to do, given the tools and history and perceptions they possess. Judging others or blaming others is just the opposite of a non-judgmental attitude and can be a defensive maneuver, i.e., get them before they get you. Judging or blaming others can be a way of not accepting responsibility for one's self. And, it is *never* a good thing for a loving relationship.

A non-judgmental attitude is closely related to the desire and willingness to listen to another (or maybe to another part of yourself). Listening is a skill that reflects many attitudes. If you only choose to listen to a limited number of people, you need to look closely at the ways you make that choice. Every time we exclude a category of people in our lives, we are limiting ourselves in one way or another. In this society, it is very common for women to be better listeners than men. This is due to many factors, including fear, but is also based on experience, practice, biological and neurological patterns, and gender-based value systems. More about this later.

Acceptance is an attitude of openness, tempered with a lack of negative judgment. Acceptance usually refers to feelings or beingness. It is different than approval. Acceptance implies "You are okay being you, just the way you are." **Acceptance is an essential element in the process of intimacy and relationship.** Approaching your partner's differences without defensiveness or the need to change him or her, can make the difference between a conflictual relationship and a loving, intimate one.

As Joe and Mary discovered, early in their process, each had many attitudes that were presenting obstacles to the relationship they wanted. Joe loved his TV and could not listen to Mary when the TV was on. She had become such a nag about the TV over the years, Joe had just turned her off the way his dad used to turn his mother off. He did not know how to please himself and her at the same time. When Joe stopped feeling like the "bad boy" and Mary stopped behaving in a parental fashion, they began talking as if they were equals. They were able to negotiate for what each wanted and learned that change can be positive, and not scary or threatening.

Valuing yourself is the primary step in valuing others. Valuing yourself is an attitude, of self-acceptance and self-promotion. Arrogance is a defensive attitude used by those who do not value themselves or others. It's a cover-up for feelings of inadequacy. Arrogance can also be a way of keeping others at a distance. Identifying feelings is a skill, requiring patience, acceptance and a willingness to learn, which requires courage and self-esteem. We sometimes have to be taught ways of examining our own feelings. Then we must find the courage to share those feelings with our partner for genuine intimacy.

Fear often dominates our lives. It may be the fear of looking stupid, sounding foolish, being hurt, or not being loved. **The fear that each of us carries around can often be summarized as the fear that we are not completely lovable,** that there is something fundamentally wrong with us that will prevent us from getting the love we want.

> *Coupling is the most profound context in which fear is manifest. It is also the arena providing the most complete opportunity for learning to believe that "Because we deserve it, we can learn to receive the love we want."*

You are a conglomeration of the world you experienced as you were growing from infancy. Many of your present attitudes were formed before you had a fully developed, rational, logical processing system to help you comprehend the situations you were facing. Nevertheless, you came to a conclusion about a given situation as well as the feelings about yourself in that situation. Your basic infant instincts were mostly based on a feeling of all or nothing, good or bad, i.e., does it work or not?

As you grew older, your attitudes formed. At the time, you couldn't analyze the reasons why you felt the way you did. You just felt! For example, as an adult, you may not understand why you hate swimming pools. You are unable to remember the experience of falling into a swimming pool when you were eight months old and almost drowned. You may be aware of the inappropriate nature of your attitude toward swimming pools but unable to understand how this attitude was developed to protect you.

This is an example of an inappropriate attitude based on an inability to properly process an early childhood experience. Incomplete processing of early childhood experiences can lead to inappropriate expectations and responses in adulthood. Similarly, you may have had a negative, ambiguous or fearful experience of a sexual nature as a very small child. You may have developed an attitude(s) about some aspect of sexuality which originally served to protect but you now find inhibiting. If attitudes are a problem in your relationship, it might be better to start with a book more specifically devoted to communication skills. You can always return to sexual issues later. Many of our attitudes are adopted from parental attitudes, especially those around intimacy and sexuality.

As an adult, you are better able to care for yourself than when you were a child. **You have the power to choose new attitudes** that appropriately reflect who you are or who you want to be. Check the list of attitudes below that promote growth to explore how many of these attitudes were present within your family, as you were growing up.

- *Acceptance of other's feelings and opinions.*
  As a child, did you feel as though Mom and Dad validated your feelings and opinions? Or, did you often feel discounted for what you felt? Do you feel wrong or bad when your partner disagrees with you? Having feelings of not being accepted as a child will promote similar feelings in interactions with your partner.

- *Non-judgmental*
  Were you praised and acknowledged for what you did rather than criticized for what you didn't do? Were you given credit just for trying? Were your parents open-minded towards your ideas, feelings, and opinions? If yes, it is probably easier for you to be less judgmental of your self, your partner, and others as an adult.

- *Desire and willingness to listen*
  The ability of parents to listen to their children, even at an early age, fosters attitudes of self-worth within a child. If your parents took the time to listen to you, you probably now feel as though your communications are important. Likewise, you have created positive attitudes around listening to your partner and others.

ATTITUDES THAT PROMOTE PERSONAL
AND RELATIONSHIP GROWTH !!

Acceptance of others' feelings and opinions,

Non-judgmental,
Desire and willingness to listen,
Playfulness,
Desire to learn and explore,
Willingness to consider new ideas and behaviors,
Courage to change,
Being responsible for own feelings, thoughts, attitudes, and behaviors.

ATTITUDES THAT DISCOURAGE PERSONAL AND RELATIONSHIP GROWTH !!

Defensiveness,
Fear,
Blaming,
Controlling, commanding,
Lack of commitment,
Lack of openness, know-it-all,
Dishonesty,
Inattention,
Inability or unwillingness to examine self,
Inability or unwillingness to share feelings and thoughts.

ATTITUDE QUESTIONNAIRE

Practice

ATTITUDES

Purpose: To discover and share your attitudes which can profoundly affect your relationship.

- **Set aside 60 minutes.**

- **Each partner will examine each of the following true/false statements one at a time. Read each statement aloud, indicate whether it is true or false for you, and discuss your feelings with your partner.**

- **Listen to your partner's responses without judgment. You may ask for clarification by saying "I don't understand."**

    1. I feel accepting and comfortable when you disagree with me.
    2. I am understanding and compassionate when you cry.
    3. When you are angry, I can listen without getting defensive.
    4. I'm able to be supportive and nurturing when you make a serious mistake.
    5. I am focused and attentive when you are talking to me.
    6. I accept your feelings whether or not I understand them.
    7. I am open to new ideas and changes in my life.
    8. It is easy for me to be light and playful.
    9. I get angry or withdraw when you criticize me.
    10. I expect you to do things my way.
    11. I frequently feel apprehensive.
    12. I'm afraid you won't love me if I disagree with you.
    13. It's usually your fault when we argue.
    14. I've difficulty committing to a process or a project.
    15. Negotiation with you is hard for me.
    16. It's hard for me to examine my feelings.
    17. I'm reluctant to share my feelings with you.
    18. Sometimes it's hard to be honest with you.

- **Which of your attitudes are facilitating feelings of intimacy?**
- **Which of your attitudes are presenting obstacles to intimacy and need to be modified?**
- **Which of the above described attitudes would you like to add to your personal repertoire?**

- **Which would you like to reduce or eliminate?**

When Craig and Sally first went through this list of attitudes, both got very depressed. "It's hopeless," sighed Sally. Craig nodded agreement. One step at a time is all anyone can do. Working on one attitude change can make a big difference. Sally found this to be true when she discovered she could choose to not be critical of Craig. She wasn't sure how it happened, but it did.

A MYTH OF RELATIONSHIP

You may have believed that, after courtship, your relationship would take care of itself as you shifted your focus to other life issues such as career or family. As you have probably figured out already, this is far from true! A relationship needs ongoing maintenance and nurturing in order to remain healthy and strong.

A relationship needs ongoing maintenance and nurturing in order to remain healthy and strong.

In preparation for the rest of this Playbook, this practice will allow you to examine the qualities each of you believes should be a part of a loving relationship.

Practice

THE BANK BOOK OF LOVING

Using the metaphor of a bank book, we each know that money cannot be taken out if we have not put money in. It is very similar in a relationship. A loving relationship with a large number of deposits, made over time, collects high rates of interest. These relationships can weather storms and cushion crises. Relationships which have meager savings will be vulnerable to the stresses and strains of everyday life with little room for error.

- **Alternating turns, each partner is to list a quality or a behavior that can be found in a loving relationship. Some examples of deposits are trust, honesty, gifting, etc.**
- **In the corresponding column, list the qualities or behaviors that can be found in a painful, dysfunctional, destructive relationship. These are the withdrawals. Some examples are anger, judgments, criticism.**
- **Use another sheet of paper if necessary.**

BANK BOOK OF LOVE

DEPOSITS	WITHDRAWALS
_____	_____
_____	_____
_____	_____
_____	_____
_____	_____
_____	_____
_____	_____
_____	_____
_____	_____

- **Look over the list you have created. Reassure yourself how much you already know about what good relationships need.**
- **Remove your sheets of paper and place them in a prominent place in your bedroom to serve as an ongoing reminder of the goals you are working on.**

There is one way the metaphor of the bank book breaks down. In your real bank book, there is a 1:1 ratio between deposits and money available for withdrawals. In a relationship, the withdrawals, i.e. the negative behaviors, have much greater weight. As a result, a couple must make 5-10 deposits for every withdrawal just to stay even. If your relationship is already in the red, you will have to increase that ratio significantly, maybe 30-50 deposits for every withdrawal to make progress and promote healing.

Remember to make deposits every day. Withdrawals need to be addressed seriously with the goal of eliminating as many as possible.

3

Communicating for Greater Intimacy

What is communication and why is it so important?

Communication is the process whereby two individuals (or more) give each other "meaning-full" messages. This can be verbal or non-verbal. In the vast majority of face-to-face communications, the non-verbal part of a communication is the most powerful. Meta-communications are those non-verbal messages which are given through tone, inflection, gesture, idiom, or other imbedded message(s). Couples use meta-communication extensively. Because these are the communications that can most easily be misinterpreted or misunderstood, it is often meta-communications which require close scrutiny.

Communication is the means by which two individuals interact emotionally. A relationship grows and flowers based on the quality of the communication. A loving relationship will grow rich and move toward greater and greater intimacy, or it will slowly wither and die. There is no middle ground. There are many dead relationships that have a social exterior, but the inside is empty. A relationship in which the two partners learn and practice intimate communication has a great vitality and resilience. The two partners grow in the context of the relationship and their love is enriched.

> **A relationship in which the two partners learn and practice intimate communication has a great vitality and resilience.**

Intimacy is not dumping your frustration, anger, disappointment, or other negative reactions on your partner. It is being honest *without* blaming the other. Telling my spouse that I am furious is not blaming. Telling him that he is a jerk, and the sole reason that I am furious, is blaming.

COMMUNICATION MYTHS

Couples often behave as if they could read each other's minds. No doubt that when two people have lived together for many years, certain habits become obvious. However, believing that you know exactly what is going on in your partner's mind can be very misleading and a setup for disaster.

Similarly, believing that your partner "should know" what you're thinking or feeling can also lead to major misunderstandings. Mind reading in any form will serve to limit intimate communication between you and your partner, therefore limiting the potential for ecstatic sex.

The belief that both partners **should want** the same things or have the same needs is also potentially destructive. No two people are alike: you grow up in different families, often in different parts of the world, with different values, rules, and expectations.

Men and women not only have different interests, they process information in different ways. As noted in the chapter on gender differences (Chapter 9), there are developmental differences in the way young boys and girls learn to talk. Girls practice verbally communicating earlier and more frequently than boys. Girls tend to talk more extensively about feelings and relationships from an earlier age. They learn as children that relationship is related to talking. Boys tend to be more oriented toward what is going on outside of themselves, e.g. games, making money, sports, etc. Boys often think that *doing* is what love is all about, *not talking*. Being sensitive to these communication differences is critical in an intimate relationship.

When couples fall in love, there is often an initial feeling of, **"we are just alike."** Early intimacy often focuses on the ways you are alike. As the relationship progresses and conflict becomes a reality, this can change rapidly. Most individuals seek validation from their partner. In other words, a partner seeks agreement as a way of reassuring him/herself that he/she is okay. So a difference of opinion or source of conflict signals a lack of validation and emotionally fuels insecurity. One partner may begin to withdrawal emotionally and begin emphasizing all the ways his partner is not like him. He begins to focus on these issues and may feel it is hopeless to believe she can ever understand him. We seek agreement for self-validation and to avoid conflict. To move beyond this need requires the maturity of "you can be you and I can be me." This can also be seen as an "agreement to disagree." This does not come easily but is a must if a relationship is to flourish.

We seek agreement for self-validation and to avoid conflict. To move beyond this need requires the maturity of "you can be you and I can be me."

Couples cannot avoid conflict because they can't avoid their differences. When two people become close and choose to be together, disagreements and arguments are inevitable. The way(s) a couple copes with disagreements will either push the relationship toward greater intimacy or toward anger, resentment, withdrawal, and self-protection. These are the only two options. Resentment, withdrawal, and self-protection are always damaging in a loving, long-term relationship.

There are only two options when conflict occurs: Protection or resolution, i.e., anger/withdrawal or greater intimacy/trust.

There are only two options when conflict occurs: Protection or resolution, i.e., anger/withdrawal or greater intimacy/trust.

TALKING FOR INTIMACY

Many people believe that telling their truth or revealing their true selves can hurt either themselves or another person. This may, indeed, happen, but a great price is paid for sacrificing the truth. The cost is decreased levels of trust and intimacy. The answer lays in looking at "your truth" in a very different way.

Think of truth as a precious gem, the most precious gift you can ever give another.

From now on, think of truth as a precious gem, the most precious gift you can ever give another. **As with any other precious gift, it's important to give it wisely and sensitively.** It's important not to give a great gift in a "hit-and-run" fashion. Although telling the truth may feel uncomfortable and scary in the moment, the net result, over time, is increased trust, intimacy and communication with your partner. Truth comes from deep inside without the intent to cause pain or guilt. **Truth is never blameful.** Truth rarely comes from an impulse; it is felt and thought, deeply.

In a loving relationship, each partner asks for what she or he wants, openly and non-judgmentally. This doesn't mean you will always get what you want, but you will feel the freedom to ask. This doesn't mean that you won't feel anxious from time to time, but fear will not immobilize you or cause you to hide. **Fear is the largest obstacle to love and intimacy.** The fears of not being pretty or rich enough, successful or sexy enough condense into one basic fear of not being good enough to be loved. That is a fear from the past that each individual must solve for him or her self. **Your partner will never be able to make you feel "Okay, enough."** This has to come from inside you.

The fear of not being good enough to be truly loved keeps many of us from asking for what we really want. Maybe you want more kisses, longer foreplay, or maybe you just want to be held close once in a while. When you don't ask for what you want, you are rejecting yourself before the other person can reject you, or more realistically, give you what you want. Tip: Always ask, even if you think the odds are against you. By asking, you push the odds in your favor and refuse to give in to your inhibiting fear. Something is always better than nothing.

Here's a tip, that if used, can provide you with much more of everything you want.

> **Orv's Law #1**
> Ask for 100% of what you want, 100% of the time.
> Be prepared to hear "No."
> **Then, negotiate the difference.**

It is, of course, unrealistic to expect that anyone is capable of asking for 100% of what they want 100% of the time, but strive for 100%. However, you will find that you get more than if you ask for only 75%. In Step 2, be prepared to hear "No," but expect to hear "Yes." Often this is translated as *expect* to hear "No," not be prepared to hear "No." It's everyone's right to choose "no" as their response.

If your partner has had a painful past, either as a child or in a relationship, he or she may be ultra-sensitive. This sensitivity can be a major obstacle to asking for what you want. Your partner may perceive your asking for what you want as a criticism. This situation requires a great deal of patience. Hearing your partner's request without defensiveness can, at first, be difficult and challenging. Remember to reassure your partner that your intention is to create a win-win situation.

In negotiating a difference, do your best to create a win-win solution. After all, 80% of what you want is better than nothing. A good lead-in statement is "Well, if you're unwilling to give me this, what would you be willing to give me?"

Love and trust give the relationship the strength to do this negotiation of desire. The converse is just as true: Doing this gives the relationship love and trust.

In addition to one's truth, there are other qualities (meta-communications) of verbal communication that are important. Are you careful about the tone of your voice? Do you sometimes imply one feeling when you are really feeling something else? This is a form of non-truth. We call it incongruence, as we saw with Craig. Perhaps it's time to walk your talk and tell your truth. Keep your tone respectful of your lover (partner). Always speak to your partner as you would your very best friend. Be cautious not to imply blame or fault.

Always speak to your partner as you would your very best friend.

Pay careful attention to this next paragraph. **If you tend to blame your partner for your feelings, two negative consequences occur:**
 1. you feel as a victim (leaving you with a sense of powerlessness; and
 2. you will resent your partner because it feels as if he/she has all the power. It is also likely your partner will begin to feel your resentment. He or she is truly powerless to affect your feelings. It is very useful for each of you to learn and remember, "I am not responsible for your thoughts, feelings, or behaviors, and you are not responsible for mine." More about this in Chapter 4.

A quick way to note if you are blaming through your tone/talk is to check to see if you are using "I" messages or "you" messages. "I" messages are sentences that begin with "I" and convey feelings, wants, or thoughts. "You" messages are sentences that begin with "you" and convey blame or attack. If you rely heavily on "you" messages, you are probably blaming more than is constructive.

Learning to use "I" messages keeps you focused on what you are feeling and doing and not what your partner is doing. Using an "I" message helps to emphasis that you have responsibility only for you and not for your partner.

Quick Tip for Talking Intimately

Learning to use "I" messages, use this formula for a start.

"I" feel _____, when
          (feeling)

you _____.
       (partner's behavior)

What I want (or would like) from you is

_____.

"You" messages imply blame and judgment. For example,

"You" are _____.
          (judgment, e.g., stupid, wrong, thoughtless)

"You" never _____
            (behavior, e.g., put toilet lid down)

When a partner is judgmental or critical of the other, love withers. The self-esteem of the recipient of those criticisms diminishes. Passing judgment on someone you love undermines the relationship and establishes or maintains a one-up, one-down situation. Many individuals are not aware of the many ways they put their partner down. It may be done with demands, helpful hints, taking over a task, a look, or a tone of voice.

You may have grown up in a dysfunctional family, where criticism was the norm. If so, you grew up believing that criticism was the only way to make the world work.

As you do the exercises in this manual, remain non-judgmental and open to new ways of seeing. You and your partner will change as you desire much more rapidly when you both use positive communications, i.e., stroking. It is also important to acknowledge and compliment yourself, to sustain your self-esteem and attitude of playfulness.

Be gentle. Set small goals and stick to them consistently. *Congratulate yourself for each new step.* As you are filled with more self-love and respect, it will add to your love for your partner. A realistic goal might be "one change for one chapter."

As you are filled with more self-love and respect, it will add to your love for your partner.

Lastly, it is important for the talker (sender of the communication) to check in with the partner (listener) regarding what is being heard. Although the sender may think he or she is being crystal clear, it may be that the partner is on a completely different track and receiving a message very different than you are intending. Checking in, i.e., asking, "What did you hear me say?" or something similar, can go a long way toward reducing miscommunications. If you have been misunderstood, you can then adjust your communication accordingly. Assuming that you have been understood by your partner when in fact you have not, is the most common problem in poor communication. It is also easy to correct. **Remember: It's the sender's responsibility to make sure he/she is understood as he/she intended.** When feelings are involved, misunderstandings run rampant. Checking in is essential.

**Remember:
It's the sender's responsibility to make sure he/she is understood as he/she intended.**

ON COACHING FROM PARTNER

If the listener, i.e., your partner, doesn't receive your intended communication, it's up to you to get feedback from her/him that will enable you to more congruently convey what you wanted to say.

Craig asked Suzanne to go to the movies. Although she said yes, the tone in her voice left Craig confused. It sounded as if she really didn't want to go, but she was saying yes. Craig then inquired, "It sounds as if you're not sure if you want to go. Please clarify." Suzanne reassured him she really wanted to go but had been preoccupied with something else when he had first asked, explaining the unusual tone in her voice.

It's important that you listen to your partner's coaching and accept his/her feedback as valid without getting defensive. This can be a point where one or the other can get stuck in the, "No I didn't, yes you did," cycle which can escalate into upset and detract from the original communication.

This can be a real challenge if your partner won't believe or accept your intention but wants to stay with her or his interpretation. If your partner will not listen to your intention and modify her/his response accordingly, there may be self-esteem issues or control issues at play.

Sally had a hard time believing Bill when he said he was sorry for not calling her when he had a late meeting at the office. He had done this before. When Bill brought this issue to the next session, a suggestion was made to help his message be more fully congruent with his words. Sally was instructed to let Bill know that she sensed his mixed message, by saying, "When you said I'm sorry, I heard the words but your voice didn't feel sincere to me. Would you please apologize again in a tone that would help me feel your sincerity." Bill had a hard time at first trusting Sally's feedback. After a few experiences he became more comfortable and was able to express his feelings more sincerely in his communications to Sally which helped her believe his intentions. **Remember: It's the sender's responsibility for assuring that the receiver receives the intended message.**

As you work with each other to improve your communication skills, you'll begin to build trust around each other's feedback.

LISTENING: A WAY TO SAY "I LOVE YOU"

Listening is a powerful way to say "I love you and respect you." Learning to listen well requires that you turn off the noise in your own head, i.e., your retorts, your opinions on the subject, your need to be agreed with, your desire to interrupt and your judgment. This can be a lot harder than you might imagine. When you are empathically listening to your partner, your only goal is to understand his or her words, context, and feelings so you may put yourself into her or his shoes, and truly empathize with her/his position.

Guidelines for Good Listening
(to be used when feelings/differences are the issue)

1. *Create Space* (or environment) with little or no interruption.

2. Each come to the discussion with the ***intention to communicate, understand*** and resolve, not judge or make wrong.

3. *Maintain eye contact* for concentration and focus. (you don't have to stare).

4. *Pay attention to your partner.* Planning your own defense reduces your ability to focus on your partner's communication.

5. *Keep body posture accepting* and open.

6. *Keep tone and volume* of voice *neutral* to promote emotional safety.

7. *No interrupting.* Let the speaker complete a train of thought. Ask if he/she is complete before talking.

8. Ask ***questions only for clarification*** *and understanding.* "I don't understand, please help me."

9. Periodically or upon request of your partner, *repeat back to your partner* what you think you heard to clarify accuracy of communication.

10. *Listen for understanding, not agreement.* Complete understanding is necessary before an agreement and/or negotiation can happen.

Although all of these points are very important, for ready reference, see below.

Quick Tip

GOOD LISTENING

1. Listen for understanding not agreement.
2. No interrupting.
3. Ask questions only for clarification and understanding.

THE MYTH OF INTIMACY

The myth of intimacy is that intimacy always takes a sweet, loving appearance. That's one side of intimacy, to be sure, but that isn't the whole package. Intimacy also encompasses the revelation of each other's "dark side." This is the most fearful side of intimacy. This is the side that we self-judge most harshly. This is the side that's hardest for most people to see as a "precious gift." When we avoid being truthful with our partner, we severely limit the intimacy possible with that partner. When you hold your partner's revealing communication as a precious gift, an *emotional safety net* is created. The receiver can appreciate what a risk the speaker is taking in delivering this very vulnerable communication and the speaker can stay present with the receiver. This means she/he is available to support and nurture the receiver through any impact the communication may have. The question for you to ask of yourself and your partner is, "What can I do to make it safer for (you) my partner to tell, or receive an intimate communication. A common challenge is knowing when your partner's communication is a risk for him or her. It is a good idea to let your partner know if you are sharing a risky feeling or thought.

Each time you risk telling your truth (feelings, opinions, etc.) and you don't feel overly judged and criticized by your partner, you'll feel safer and more able to risk further next time. By taking successfully deeper and deeper leaps into truth and intimacy, love grows stronger. **When love is strong and you feel loveable, sex can be more passionate.** Needless to say, the converse is true.

Intimacy also encompasses the revelation of each other's "dark side." This is the most fearful side of intimacy.

NURTURING COMMUNICATION

We all need to be nurtured and most of us want to be nurtured. Many of us don't even know what nurturing is. When you feel nurtured, what is communication and why is it so important?

Communication is the process whereby two individuals (or more) give each other *meaning-full* messages. This can be verbal or non-verbal. In the vast majority of face-to-face communications, the non-verbal part of a communication is the most powerful. Meta-communications are those non-verbal messages which are given through tone, inflection, gesture, idiom or other imbedded message(s). Couples use meta-communication extensively. Because these are the communications that can most easily be misinterpreted or misunderstood, it is often meta-communications which require close scrutiny.

In the vast majority of face-to-face communications, the non-verbal part of a communication is the most powerful.

When Craig felt criticized by Sally, he would become very quiet. His face would get red, but he would verbally deny he was angry or upset when questioned by Sally. Sally would then get enraged because she sensed the incongruity and felt that Craig wasn't telling her the truth. Needless to say, this conflict would often escalate and end with feelings of alienation and distance. The reality is that Craig could not readily recognize his feelings. Through their therapy, Craig and Sally were better able to recognize the multiple messages they were sending each other. They learned alternative ways of interpreting and responding, leading to more emotional trust and improved communication between them. Craig had to work very hard to identify his feelings. Sally had to examine the source of her rage.

You can have love without intimacy and you can have intimacy without love, although one without the other tends to be time limited. When you communicate with your lover (partner) honestly, trust flourishes with understanding and acceptance. Intimacy deepens and love continues to grow. Communicating for intimacy includes honesty and has elements which have been examined in the course of this chapter. In some sense intimacy is communication. It is the communication about your inner self with acute awareness of your self in the presence of another person, i.e., your partner. Intimacy may be painful, anxiety producing, exhilarating, difficult or easy, but the relationship moves forward on the basis of it. Intimacy may promote closeness or may lead the couple toward the ending of a relationship. Regardless of the long-term results, a couple cannot have closeness for long if the intimacy is not there.

You can have love without intimacy and you can have intimacy without love, although one without the other tends to be time limited.

When Sherry asked Jim to be more nurturing in his communication, Jim had no idea what she meant. Sherry was able to explain that she wanted Jim to touch her gently when they spoke and to make eye contact with her and acknowledge her by listening intently. She carefully explained how she felt shut out and unimportant when he did not look at her during their discussions. Although afraid he might not be able to do it, Jim tried these new behaviors. He found Sherry more open and receptive to him as a result. Jim learned more ways to support Sherry by asking interesting and stimulating questions. This was all new to him because he had no model in his life for this kind of behavior. Because Jim was recognizing and enjoying the payoff for himself, he asked her if there were other ways he could support her. Sherry began to feel more free and less judged in her communication with Jim. She was able to share with him more ideas about ways he could nurture her. Because she felt nurtured, she was able to be more nurturing toward Jim, maintaining the circle of respect, caring, and acknowledgment, the basis of a solid relationship.

Nurturing communication fosters a sense of closeness and coziness. It can be a compliment. It can be attention given for just being you. It is acknowledgment of anything positive. Any communication that feels nurturing is nurturing, whether it is spoken or written. It may be the words, but more than likely it is the tone, the facial expression, and the body language, that communicates the loving meaning and intent.

Nurturing communications can be intimate communications and often are. Intimate communications may not feel nurturing at the time given, although they may lead to greater nurturing and feelings of support in the long run.

Practice

THE RESENTMENT PROCESS

    Purpose: The purpose of this practice is to create a safe context in which to bring up any old hurts or resentments that may be blocking deeper intimacy. The listener has an opportunity to own the impact of his/her behavior on the speaker.

    Time: 45 minutes for the practice and discussion afterwards.

Directions:

- **Sit comfortably, face to face, making eye contact.**

- **Choose who will be the first speaker and the partner will be the listener.**
- **Each person will have 15 minutes in each role before switching roles.**

1. The speaker begins by thinking of a hurt, anger or resentment triggered by something the other person said or did.

2. The speaker starts by saying, "I felt _____
   (hurt, angry, resentful, frustrated, helpless, etc.)

   when you _____."
   (partner's behavior)

3. The receiver replies by saying, "Thank you, I hear that."

4. Next, the speaker asks for a different course of action or behavior for similar future incidents.

5. The listener owns the impact of his/her behavior on the speaker by saying, I understand how that impacted your life. I'm sorry. My intention wasn't to hurt you. I am willing (or not willing) to _____."
   (new behavior)

6. If the listener isn't willing to change in the way the speaker wishes, they may negotiate a mutually acceptable alternative behavior.

7. The listener then says, "Please forgive me for _____
   (old behavior)

   and I forgive myself for _____."
   (old behavior)

8. The speaker brings up another hurt, anger or resentment and the same process is repeated. (Repeat steps 1 through 7.)

9. At the end of 15 minutes, switch positions so the other person has a chance to share his/her hurts.

10. At the end of the next 15 minutes, stop, give each other a hug, and thank them for their participation.

11. Discuss feelings or thoughts that may have come up during the exercise. This may be lengthy if strong negative feelings arise.

Remember this is not a practice to make anyone wrong or right. It is a practice to allow each partner to more clearly appreciate and understand the impact your behavior has on your partner. The second purpose is to clarify intent. The intent in a loving relationship is not to hurt your partner but to understand and support.

Remember, the key to this practice is to own (take responsibility for) the impact of your behavior on your partner and to ask for forgiveness and forgive yourself for the behavior that triggered pain with your partner.

USE THE ABOVE FORMAT WORD FOR WORD to guide you. For optimal results, avoid discussing issues that were brought up. Please don't use the information to verbally beat up on yourself or your partner. This is only to increase mutual understanding.

4

Rescue in Relationship or How to Ruin a Good Relationship Fast

Rescuing your partner or yourself results in both partners feeling victimized, angry and distant. The person doing the rescuing is assuming his/her partner is unable to take care of her/himself or is in some way in a one-down position, i.e., powerless. The rescuer becomes a caretaker. The person being rescued loses an opportunity to learn or expand his/her limits or abilities. The rescued person may feel victimized or angry as a result. In every case, the act of rescuing reaffirms and maintains the power imbalance between partners.

OPPORTUNITIES FOR RESCUE TO OCCUR

1. Any situation in which one partner does something for the other partner that he or she can do for themselves.
   Example: A wife who picks up her husband's clothes that have been thrown around their bedroom rather than put in the hamper. It bothers her, but she doesn't say anything to her husband until she becomes angry enough to explode at him.

2. Any situation in which one partner does something that he or she does not want to do in relation to his/her partner.
   Example: A partner who participates in an event that she/he really doesn't like, but doesn't let the other person know. The result is that the partner continues doing the same activity. The anger and resentment build without the "offending" partner knowing she/he is offending.

3. Any situation in which one partner does something for the other without that partner asking for help.
   Example: A partner "taking over" a task or project because she/he is afraid their partner won't do it well enough or that it's taking too long. The result is the partner doesn't get the practice to become more proficient and may feel resentful or patronized.

4. A partner not asking for what she/he wants because of being afraid of his/her partner's reaction, or the belief that she/he cannot really get it.
   Example: One partner wants to go to a special resort, but thinks his/her partner will angrily object. She/he goes along with his/her partner's recommendation. This sets up the non-asking partner for resentment and the other partner remains in ignorance.
   Reminder — Ask for 100% of what you want 100% of the time.

5. A situation in which a partner isn't being honest or is withholding information around what is bothering him/her or what he/she would like the partner to do differently.
   Example: One partner is feeling angry or resentful towards their partner but is "stuffing" the feelings rather than communicating their feelings because of the fear of the partner's response. This results in the first partner holding onto feelings that block closeness and creates distance. The second partner may not be aware of the impact of his/her action and is in a powerless position to either get closer or take responsibility for his/her behavior.

6. Any joint activity in which one partner puts in more effort or more interest than the other partner.
   Example: A couple agrees to paint a room in their house. Soon after they begin the project, one partner loses interest and the other partner spends the better part of the day completing the project. The partner having to

finish the project will most likely feel angry and manipulated. By finishing the project, she/he has rescued the partner from taking responsibility for their initial agreement.

The act of rescuing reaffirms and maintains the power imbalance between partners.

When an individual is rescued, it may feel good in the moment, but she/he soon feels powerless and victimized. No one likes to think of themself as incompetent, powerless, or victimized at the hands of another. We may feel humiliated or enraged at the rescuer who has unwittingly colluded with our sense of powerlessness. One way to stop "rescues" is to ask for honesty from your partner and others. (See Chapter 3 on Communicating for Intimacy and the Relationship Ripple in Chapter 5 for more about honesty.)

Both rescuer and the rescued may have a hard time learning to speak her/his truth and not feel guilty while refusing to take responsibility for how his/her partner may feel as a result. This is a very critical issue: **Do not take what your partner says personally.** It can be helpful to remember that his/her behavior or words reflect his/her "stuff," not yours. You're okay, just the way you are.

A partner who receives an ego boost from taking care of his/her partner will be very disappointed and angry when the one rescued becomes rebellious or passive aggressive. **Rescuing is a lose-lose situation.**

Although there is a cultural bias that says men rescue women more frequently, it is interesting to note that men and women rescue differently. Women tend to rescue men regarding emotional issues. Men tend to rescue women for more physical issues, i.e., household projects, career decisions, etc.

Practice

RESCUE

> **Purpose:** To discover the various ways that you may be rescuing each other in your relationship.

Give yourself thirty minutes to complete the practice.
Each partner is to consider the six methods of rescue listed below.

- **Write down the various ways each of you rescue under the appropriate method of rescue and the ways each of you feels rescued. You will each have two lists.**
- **When both of you have completed your lists, share them with each other.**
- **Discuss ways and make agreements that will support the elimination of rescues in your relationship. This may require more than one discussion.**

1. Any situation in which one person does something for the other that the person can do for themselves.

   I rescue when:

   I feel rescued when:

2. Any situation in which one person does something that he or she does not want to do in relation to his/her partner.

   I rescue when:

   I feel rescued when:

3. Any situation in which one person does something for the other without that person asking for help.

4. A partner who does not ask for what he/she wants because of fear of partner's reaction, or the belief that he/she can't really have it.

5. A situation(s) in which a partner isn't being honest or is withholding information around what is bothering him/her or what he/she would like the partner to do differently.

6. Any joint activity in which one person puts in more effort or more interest than the other partner.

You each now have two lists. Focus on one method of rescue at a time and describe for your partner exactly what you have meant in your description. Ask your partner for verbal feedback so you can be sure he or she understands what you have described. It might be helpful for you to go over how you rescue and see if it agrees with your partner's feelings of being rescued.

THE THIN LINE BETWEEN RESCUE
AND AUTHENTIC SUPPORT

When a person rescues his/her partner, she/he is contributing to keeping that person ignorant, powerless or one-down. This may not be a conscious intention, but thwarts the opportunity to increase truth, trust, and intimacy levels. A couple cannot reach deeper levels of intimacy and sexuality if rescue is present in the relationship.

In contrast, **authentic support empowers your partner** to take care of her/himself and to ensure her/his own growth in the learning process. Not rescuing may bring discomfort, fear of rejection, or retaliation, for instance, when you courageously tell a truth that you know will upset your partner because you know the truth will be best for the relationship. Although most rescues come from the loving intention of "I was just trying to help you," the overall result is to destroy the relationship and disempower the partner.

Authentic support promotes growth. Rescue promotes powerlessness, conflict, and stagnation in relationship.

Authentic support is being there physically, emotionally, and spiritually for your partner, but letting him/her have his/her own experience. Let your partner supply his/her own answers. It's offering a hand, but not taking over. It's truly believing that your partner is capable of taking care of him/herself. It's your partner knowing that you are there for them if you are needed.

When you are being honest with your thoughts, feelings, wants, and desires, you are empowering your partner to grow by doing the same. Authentic support promotes growth. Rescue promotes powerlessness, conflict, and stagnation in relationship. By deciding not to rescue each other, you will be taking a big step in deepening the personal growth in each of you and moving toward greater intimacy and hotter sexuality in your relationship.

How is this related to sex? For example, if you treat your partner/spouse as if they can't do anything right, you will lose respect for her/him. Are you going to be turned on to someone you don't respect? Similarly, if you are the one who is disempowered, are you going to want to be sexual with anyone?

There is always the assumption made by the rescuer that the other partner is in some way unable to take care of her/himself, or isn't quite as clever, smart, or talented as one's self. In every case, the act of rescuing another person reaffirms and maintains this one-up, one-down power imbalance between the rescuer and the victim and prevents the possibility of people becoming equals in a relationship. In order to eliminate rescues, one has to believe that your partner is capable of taking care of him/herself. Rescuing diminishes the potential for intimacy. Believing in the need and right of each human being to respect and acceptance fosters the environment in which true intimacy can grow.

When a partner is judgmental or critical of the other, love withers. The self-esteem of the recipient of those criticisms diminishes. Passing judgment on someone you love undermines the relationship and creates a one-up, one-down situation. Many individuals are not aware of the many ways they put their partner down. It may be done with demands, helpful hints, taking over a task, a look, or a tone of voice.

You may have grown up in a dysfunctional family, where criticism was the norm. If so, you grew up believing that criticism was the only way to support your partner and to make the world work.

As you do the exercises in this manual, remain non-judgmental and open to new ways of seeing. You and your partner will change in the direction you desire much more rapidly when you both use positive communications, i.e. reinforcements. It is also important to acknowledge and compliment yourself, to sustain your self-esteem and attitude of playfulness. People learn quicker in an atmosphere of appreciation, not criticism. There is no room in a loving relationship for criticism.

Be gentle. **Set small goals and stick to them consistently.** Congratulate yourself for each new step. As you are filled with more self-love and respect, it will add to your love for your partner. Stroking or acknowledgment is an art and can be learned with focus and practice. See Chapter 6.

Believing in the need and right of each human being to respect and acceptance fosters the environment in which true intimacy can grow.

5

Emotional Intimacy for Going Deeper

Emotional intimacy is the ability of the "real" you to be in touch with your "real" partner. This means both partners are open to their soft, vulnerable inner cores. For this to happen, you must feel emotionally strong, courageous and safe. It takes time and risk to build the trust necessary to open to deeper and deeper levels with your partner.

The Relationship Ripple, illustrated below, shows how the various components of relationship (whether with yourself or another)

Relationship Ripple

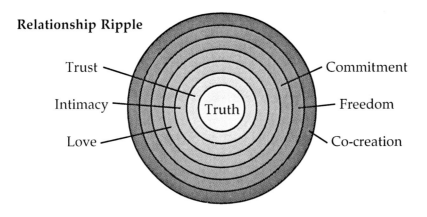

build upon each other to build strong, healthy relationships. We'll discuss how each flows and builds upon the other.

When you are confronting or speaking your truth, your partner, over time, will begin to trust you more. Your integrity level rises. The partner's trust level grows stronger. If there is a feeling of general reciprocation, trust builds on both sides. This reciprocation might not be true for each situation, but there must be a feeling of effort coming from each partner. As each partner becomes more trusting of the other, the invitation to move to deeper levels of intimacy is given. It may be surprising to you to see "Love" in the ripple beyond Truth, Trust, and Intimacy. Without these three core components, however, love will only be a hollow shell of the real thing.

Emotional and physical intimacy are enhanced by each other. Emotional intimacy is a necessary requisite for physical intimacy. Emotional intimacy comes from the willingness to be open and honest with each other. In-ti-ma-cy can phonetically be translated to "Into me you see." The components of an intimate relationship are truth, trust, intimacy, love, commitment, freedom, and co-creation.

Truth

To first access and then communicate your honest feelings or thoughts sets the stage for trust, vulnerability, and intimacy. This is the hardest step for most of us. You may not know what you want, what you feel, or what you believe. You may be masking your real truth to please your partner, Mom, Dad, church or other important people in your lives. The fear of rejection, anger, or hurting your partner can prompt you to withhold information and feelings, i.e., emotional withhold. (See Rescue, Chapter 4.)

Your truth (honesty) is the most precious gift you can give your partner. By not telling your partner what you are thinking, feeling, or wanting, you are denying him/her the opportunity to know the real you. When you hold back, you start to distrust yourself and your partner. Without truth, there can be little vulnerability or intimacy. Without truth, you will never feel completely loved.

To be willing to communicate your truth, you must have confidence in your self and your partner. It is essential that you feel physically safe. This means that, in the presence of your partner, you must know you will be received without threat. You need to believe and feel that you will not be made to feel wrong, sick, dumb, crazy, perverted, or in any way not accepted. This does not mean that anger and hurt cannot emerge. If both partners are working on their relationship, these feelings can be worked through.

Without truth, you will never feel completely loved.

Reminder: Although your partner may not agree with you, it is important to know that your partner will not make you responsible for his/her feelings, i.e., not blame you for the way he/she feels. This is a critically necessary concept to understand and put into practice.

There is no magical or easy path to accessing and communicating your truth to your partner. Your courage and willingness to risk openness will play vital roles. By starting with the least emotionally charged issues, you will develop experience and trust with each other.

Trust

Trust grows naturally as a result of knowing that what you hear from your partner reflects the real him or her. There are no secrets or hidden agendas. The more you trust your partner and yourself, the more open and vulnerable you allow yourself to be. Integrity describes a high level of trustworthiness. Integrity flourishes as a result of keeping agreements and maintaining consistent behavior patterns.

Building trust is partly a function of time. If any kind of trust has been broken or violated, you will need time to rebuild.

We often think trust is something we feel for another. However, you must trust yourself for interpersonal trust to develop. High self-esteem includes trust in your self-worth, regardless of what your partner says or does (see Chapter 9, Self-Esteem). This is not to be confused with arrogance.

> **Integrity flourishes as a result of keeping agreements and maintaining consistent behavior patterns.**

Vulnerability

As you become more comfortable with telling your truth and trusting yourself and your partner on deeper levels, you will find yourself becoming more open and intimate.

Many people see vulnerability as a position of weakness, an Achilles Heel. We believe that to be open and vulnerable is really a position of *Power*. **To be vulnerable requires strength and courage.** To be vulnerable is to be open to and aware of all your feelings, from ecstasy to despair.

There can be many fears as one approaches intimacy. These fears can be summarized: "If I share all my truths with my partner, how can he or she really love me?" and/or "will he or she use my truths to hurt me?" **Deep inside many adults is a small, scared child** who is convinced that he or she has some very bad parts. These feelings result when mom and dad did not always show their love. It is hopeful that by the time you have gone through all twenty-five chapters of this playbook, you will be much closer to being able to believe and say to yourself, "I am truly lovable."

New behaviors reflect new beliefs, and new behaviors can precede new beliefs and feelings. Anything new can be felt as threatening or scary. The initial response to a new idea is often "no." Give yourself and your partner verbal and emotional support to stay open while trying new behaviors.

Love

You may be quite surprised to find *love* so far from the center of the relationship ripple. The previous components must be in place in order for one to be truly loving or "in love." For our purpose, we'll define love as: dignity, respect, understanding of another's wants, feelings, desires, and trust. This may sound a bit clinical or not very romantic, but it has the components necessary to celebrate and honor another human being.

Commitment

Commitment is a word that brings fear to the hearts of many men and women. It seems to carry with it the connotation of being "locked in" or frozen in a relationship until "death do us part." In fact, one can only commit in the present. If both partners are fully present and 100% committed to each other **in the moment**, there will be a natural desire to "re-enlist" for tomorrow, the next month, and the years to come. The very best way to get a lifetime commitment is to be fully committed to your partner and to the relationship today, with no specific expectation for the future. The future will take care of itself, when you take care of the present.

The future will take care of itself, when you take care of the present.

Freedom

By the time one reaches this point in the relationship ripple, the stage is set for a new level of freedom. It is paradoxical in that you may feel almost single again, but at the same time feel more deeply bonded than ever. This is because all the previous levels of the relationship ripple have brought you to this point. From this point, one partner can support the other to expand and express themselves free from enmeshment, knowing your relationship is safe and secure.

Co-Creation

From this point in a relationship, a couple can use their talents and abilities in a "synergistic" way. Each partner finds themselves in alignment and harmony with the other. The total of your energies together is greater than the sum of the individual energies. A couple may also choose areas to focus on within their relationship, such as raising healthy children, creating a certain level of material lifestyle, or even a greater sex life.

OPENING THE HEART

The decision to remain emotionally closed is usually derived from prior experience of pain, either in childhood and/or other love relationships. This pain may feel like rejection, abandonment, or being "bombed" by your partner. Although the trigger is in the present situation, the emotional response is based on an historical event. Because we want to avoid this old pain, many of us hide ourselves and only say or do things that we believe will be acceptable to the other. In other words, we take no risk. This is a form of rescue. Your partner, in turn, may be doing the same thing to you. The outcome is that neither person gets to know the other "real person." Intimacy is lost! Growth does not occur. The relationship fades.

The way to protect that soft, vulnerable core and build trust, which generates greater intimacy, is a slow process of self-evaluation. "I'll show you a little bit of me if you show me a little bit of you." Start with low impact information and observe how the other person is receiving it. If it is received sensitively, and openly, a sense of emotional safety and trust will result. This creates an opportunity for the other person to respond at the same level or a little deeper level of intimacy. With time, as trust builds, the sense of emotional safety and comfort increases to permit much deeper levels of self and intimate others. Warning! This isn't a journey for everyone! It takes a tremendous amount of courage and desire to push through the pitfalls and hazards that stand in the way of deeper levels of intimacy. **The pay-off is a deep, emotional connection, and the potential for emotional ecstasy and red hot sex.**

When Jon and Maria came to counseling after twenty years of marriage, they discovered that they had never been truthful about their feelings about sex. Maria was afraid, early in their marriage, to ask for what she wanted sexually. She had learned to suppress her desires out of fear. Jon's current erectile problem was directly related to not giving sex and intimacy enough attention. With a lot of ups and downs, they began to tell withheld truths. A new depth of love and closeness emerged, and sex became better than it had been in twenty years, or maybe ever. They had begun to see each other in a different light.

Practice

TRUST

> **Purpose:** To strengthen your trust for each other in preparation for new levels of emotional intimacy.

- Give yourselves at least 30 minutes (15 minutes each) in which you can totally focus on each other.
- Sit comfortably facing each other.
- One person will start by reading and answering the questions below.
- The listener will not interrupt except for clarification, i.e., "I don't understand, please tell me more."
- When the speaker feels complete with the question, she/he will say, "I'm complete," and the listener will become the speaker and repeat the above steps.

1. Areas in which I trust myself most are (honest with money, sexual desires, good cook, responsible lover, etc.)

   _____

2. Areas in which I trust myself least are (not coming home on time, inconsiderate, not losing my temper, etc.)

   _____

   What can I do about this? Am I willing to change?:

   _____

   Ways you can support me are (reminders, notes, signals, etc.):

   _____

3. Areas in which I trust you most are:

   _____

4. Areas in which I trust you least are:

   _____

   What I want to do about these areas, and how you can support me are:

   _____

5. What I need from you in order to relax and feel more sexual is:

   _____

   (more talking, consistency, more touching, less grabbing, etc.)

By periodically returning to this exercise, you can further strengthen the trust, intimacy, and understanding between you.

6

Emotional Support and Stroking

Emotional support is the process by which you feel less alone and in partnership with someone. The feeling of strength, when you know you and your partner are on the same team, is unparalleled.

Learning to accept your partner's feelings is the foundation for showing and feeling support. When you accept another's feelings, you are not approving or agreeing. Feelings are deep human responses and cannot be judged. You may want to agree or approve of a behavior, but a feeling is just a feeling, nothing more. Feelings are not right or wrong—they just are. When each of you can accept the humanness of your partner, you are well on the way to a truly intimate and dynamic relationship.

Feelings are not right or wrong—they just are.

Eric Berne, the founder of Transactional Analysis, created the concept of a "stroke." He defined a stroke as the basic unit of social interaction or recognition of another human being. Strokes can be positive or negative depending on whether they feel good or bad.

Strokes can be verbal, non-verbal, or physical (touch, body language). For the rest of this playbook, stroking will refer to positive stroking.

Compliments and acknowledgments are two common strokes which let us know we are appreciated. "Positive stroking" is a term often used to communicate emotional support. These demonstrations of emotional support are great gifts to your partner.

When many of us were growing up, we received more criticisms (negative strokes) than positive strokes. Criticisms feel punishing, often demeaning. These negative messages prevented the growth of our self-esteem as we came to believe they were true. As we grew to adulthood, it became almost impossible to receive a positive stroke. We didn't believe we deserved it. Parents raised in the early part of the century often considered it inappropriate, vain or self-centered to accept a compliment. Parents often believed complimenting or praising a child led to spoiling the child. As a result, we often grew up with clever ways to dodge and discount compliments. Perhaps you believe you must be perfect to be worthy of receiving a compliment. As a result of these kinds of beliefs, many adults give compliments rarely and have an even harder time receiving them.

Tom was a hard worker and a good provider for his wife, Joan, and their three children. There were times he put in long hours and came home exhausted. Joan had a hard time acknowledging Tom's efforts because of disappointment at not having more quality time with Tom.

The disappointment grew into resentment, then distance and anger. The anger came out in Joan's criticism of Tom for minor reasons. Sometimes Joan would berate Tom, "You never spend time with me. Do you have to spend so much time at work. You don't care about me." Tom would fire back, "Well, maybe if you would work, even part-time, I wouldn't have to work so hard. I'm only doing it for you and the kids anyway. If I were single, I wouldn't be working this hard."

Tom interpreted these actions from Joan as non-supportive and bitchy. As a result Tom spent even more time at work where he felt safe from Joan's criticism.

After several sessions Joan and Tom began to see how they had both stopped acknowledging each other early in the relationship.

They no longer felt close to one another. After much negotiation, both agreed to give at least three strokes a day to each other.

At the next session both Tom and Joan reported feeling closer and in more communication with each other. Tom was glowing as he related how good he felt on a Tuesday evening when Joan thanked him for being willing to work so hard to make such a comfortable home for her and the children. Tom acknowledged Joan with a beautiful card and a bouquet of flowers for all the attention and hard work she put into maintaining their beautiful home. Joan related that she felt as though she was being courted again. They were off to a good start.

Although we may take in thousands of bits of information that are pleasing to us about our surroundings and the people in our world, we often neglect to verbalize those pleasurable feelings or thoughts. When we miss these opportunities to stroke, we may be reducing overall closeness and intimacy in our relationship. You may also be creating roadblocks to happiness.

When we miss these opportunities to stroke, we may be reducing overall closeness and intimacy in our relationship.

When you pay attention to your pleasurable feelings and reactions and choose to share them with your partner, you are on the road to greater intimacy, deeper love, and hotter sex.

RECEIVING A STROKE

The receiver of a stroke has a challenging task. When your partner compliments or acknowledges you, you must first hear it and take a moment to absorb it. Stop the discounting thought in your mind. Take a deep breath and say "thank you." Remember, the giver is simply sharing his/her pleasurable perception of you, even if you feel or see yourself differently. **The more you acknowledge compliments, the better you will feel about receiving them, and the more you will believe them.**

For people who come from stroke-deprived childhoods, i.e., a childhood where there were predominately put-downs rather than positive strokes, it's often helpful to break strokes into the following three categories: *doing, being,* and *physical appearance.* The *doing* stroke is for something that a person has done, i.e., "Thanks, darling, for doing the dishes for me. I really appreciate your taking the time to do them." The *being* stroke is about a virtue or the way a person is. "I love your warm and gentle ways, or I love you just because you're you," are examples. The *physical appearance* stroke is a communication about how a person looks or dresses, i.e., "Honey, that suit looks great on you. The color works well with your dark, wavy hair."

Practice

EMOTIONAL STROKING

Purpose: To increase awareness of your feelings and promote the practice of giving and receiving strokes and acknowledgments.

When you are receiving, be open and take the compliment (stroke) with a deep breath and a genuine "thank you." Feel the appreciation of the gift. When you are giving, maintain eye contact with your partner.

- **Facing each other, touching if it feels comfortable, tell your partner about a recent behavior (a *DOING* stroke) that you appreciated.**
- **The receiving partner is to take in the stroke and say, "Thank you," without thinking of a reason for it not being true.**
- **Share with your partner how it felt giving the compliment. Have your partner share how it felt receiving the compliment.**
- **Reverse roles. The sender becomes the receiver and the receiver becomes the sender.**

REPEAT the above process with a compliment focusing on a personality characteristic (a *BEING* stroke); don't forget the sharing of feelings.

REPEAT the process above with a stroke focusing on a physical characteristic (a *PHYSICAL APPEARANCE* stroke).

PART II: SELF STROKING

Each of you will have an opportunity to give yourself a stroke.

- **The first partner will give a compliment to his or herself, pause, and take it in, e.g., "Sally I like your hair" or "I like my hair." Try using both the first person and the second person. Does it feel different?**
- **Share with your partner how it felt doing this.**
- **Repeat this process with a *DOING* stroke, a *BEING* stroke and a *PHYSICAL APPEARANCE* stroke.**
- **Change roles and the listening partner becomes the self-stroking partner. Repeat.**

Because stroking is so vital to emotional health, it is recommended that you use this process as a means to purposefully acknowledge (stroke) each other daily.

Strokes are a major "lubrication" of relationship. This means that even when things aren't going smoothly, strokes will help maintain a more positive and uplifting atmosphere for the two of you. If you remember to "crank up" the strokes for your partner, you'll be creating good will and keeping the channels of communication open. You'll also notice that you will feel much better as a result of acknowledging your partner.

Strokes are a major "lubrication" of relationship.

HINT: If you look for the negative, i.e., what's wrong, you'll find more negative. If you look for the positive and acknowledge it to yourself and your partner, you'll have more positive pleasure in your life, because you are focusing on the positive.

7

Passion in Everyday Life

Passion is a range of emotions experienced with intensity. We can feel love with a passion, or anger with a passion. We may feel passionate about our work and/or passionate about our partner. We believe that passion can be consciously created. To know how to create and foster passion, you must know the components of passion.

Remember when you and your partner were first in love. You couldn't seem to keep your hands off of each other. Touching, kissing, talking, and other demonstrations of your attraction and feelings for each other were always present. It felt wonderful! You believed those feelings would go on forever, would never go away. However, feelings do change. This is to be expected. As you play your way through this manual, you will learn ways of re-creating and maintaining the flavor of that original excitement, year after year. You are what you think (and perceive) and so is your partner and your relationship (see Chapter 20).

If you are sexual with your partner with the same routine, the same moves, at the same time of day and on the same day of each week, not only will you get bored, your sexual desire will diminish, regardless of the other variables that stay the same. Because **sexuality is such a critical element of the "glue" which holds couples together,** it is important to make it a priority in your relationship. A definition of "priority" is the time you give something.

Passion is a way of living, not just in sexual moments. Examine your passion while noting the elements in your life and in your relationship that contribute to creating and maintaining passion.

ELEMENTS OF PASSION

1. *Promote Fun and Excitement*

    This is a person or activity that you know you'll enjoy. You eagerly anticipate being with the person or doing the activity. Karen looks forward to each ski season with excitement. She skis often because she feels so alive when she skis.

2. *Experience Novelty*

    There are elements of the person or event that are not repetitious. There's a sense of newness or freshness.

    Margaret and Don took responsibility for adding a new element to each sexual encounter. Sometimes it was a new word, a new fantasy (or a small change in an old one), a new costume, etc. After fifteen years of marriage, they felt anticipation and appreciation of the newness of their time together.

3. *Challenge Yourself*

    Because the person or activity is not static nor always predictable, your interest and enthusiasm remain high. There's excitement in wondering what's next! How am I going to react or feel?

    Carrie was initially apprehensive when George suggested adding adult videos to their sexual stimulation. He made sure that the first one was not extreme. Carrie learned to trust his judgment, found herself turned on and looking forward to the next video. She was glad she had taken the challenge to try something new.

4. *Explore New Ideas and Activities*

    Keeping a steady flow of new ideas and activities promotes a sense of aliveness, intensity and excitement. Helen and Stan found that reading erotica aloud to each other not only was a turn-on but provided them with an ongoing potpourri of ideas. Sometimes they would try the new ideas, sometimes not. Either way it was fun to talk about the new material as a way of finding out more about each other's feelings and reactions.

Many couples find that taking classes together or studying a topic of mutual interest of a non-sexual nature keeps their minds alive and challenged. Their passion for living is renewed. This passion carries over into all aspects of their lives.

5. *Use All the Senses*

The more fully you can incorporate the five senses, the more alive and stimulating the relationship will be. Richard and Shirley found their sex life boring and mundane after fourteen years of marriage. By using the "Visiting Royalty" practice in Chapter 25, they learned how to create beautiful new settings within their bedroom to reflect different themes and moods. Both experimented with new scents and attire to feel more exotic and alluring. They also learned to spend more time touching each other's entire body in tender ways every day.

6. *Risk Beyond Your Comfort Zone*

Betty never told Frank how much she enjoyed anal penetration with previous lovers because she was afraid Frank would think she was perverted or dirty. After four years of marriage, she was able to broach the subject by talking about a third person's experience. To her surprise, Frank was interested and receptive. She then felt much more comfortable, suggesting they might mutually explore this new area of sexuality during their next love-making session. She also found the courage to share with him her excitement and overcame her fears of sharing new things with him.

7. *Thinking Youthfully*

Sex is for young folks of all ages! Keeping sex alive as you grow older will keep you feeling youthful and alive. Ralph and Margaret rekindled their sex life in their mid-sixties by using the techniques in this book which helped them focus on playfulness and the non-performance aspects of their sexuality. Their new agenda is to have fun with each other without being goal-oriented. Both report feeling younger and more energetic, not only in their love sessions, but in other areas of their lives as well. They also comment that it is the bext sex of their entire lives.

8. *Be Playful*

Paul and Jenny learned to laugh, talk, and play throughout sex by not taking themselves so seriously. **They just stopped trying to "do it right."** They were more willing to be spontaneous and explore without worrying about how they might look or sound, or where they were going. Although this is not easy, it is profoundly rewarding. If the two of you agree, it is even better.

The little boy or girl inside all of us is naturally playful, curious, and knows no shame. A large part of hot sex can flow from this little girl or boy. Our passion comes from that inner boy or girl.

The more of the above components you can identify within your life or your relationship, the more passion you'll be experiencing. Creating passion in all areas of your life will effect the passion in your sex life. Throughout this manual, we'll show you how to build the passion you want by using these components.

Creating passion in all areas of your life will effect the passion in your sex life.

Practice

CREATING PASSION

Purpose: To identify elements of passion currently present in your life and those which you might wish to add.

1. Think back to a time when you felt passionate with/about your partner. Which of the above elements of passion were present at that time in your life?

NOTES

Man	Woman
(List examples of passion components)	

_____ _____

_____ _____

_____ _____

_____ _____

_____ _____

_____ _____

_____ _____

_____ _____

2. Describe specific *examples* of each element (attitudes, behaviors, or activities) that were present in the past.

NOTES

Man	Woman
(List examples of passion components)	

_____ _____

_____ _____

_____ _____

_____ _____

_____ _____

_____ _____

_____ _____

_____ _____

3. Which of the elements are present in your life now? How are they in your life now? Be specific. Write them down, e.g., jogging, eating chocolate, flirting, buying a new _____.

NOTES

<u>Man</u>   <u>Woman</u>
(List examples of passion components)

_____   _____
_____   _____
_____   _____
_____   _____
_____   _____
_____   _____
_____   _____
_____   _____

4. Share your three lists with your partner.
5. How many items on each other's lists do you share in common?
6. Discuss any surprises or significant areas.
7. Which of the elements of passion (as you've described them) would you like to bring back into your life?
8. Discuss the major obstacles that are keeping you from having more passion in your life and/or your relationship. (Most couples find time, children, work and home to be primary obstacles.)
9. Each partner, choose an element of passion you would like to focus on in your life. Choose one way you could increase that passionate element in your life now (by overcoming an obstacle).

Man	Woman
_____	_____

(It's okay if you have the same one—or different ones.)

10. a) As a couple, choose an element of passion you'd like to focus on in your relationship. (You may have to negotiate.)

    b) Describe the way(s) you are going to make this happen.

_____
(Element of passion on which to focus)

Practice

TURN ON LIST

1. Take some time to think of ten activities in your life (not limited to sexual) that turn you on the most. Write them down.

2. After listing, jot down the number of hours you're involved in these activities throughout a typical week. Are you happy with the amount of time you are spending on these?

3. Each partner, list neatly on a separate piece of paper his/her activities.

4. Put this list in some conspicuous place in your living space so that you can review them regularly, with the intention of doing more of all the items on your list.

5. You will notice that by increasing the time spent doing these stimulating activities in your life, your passion will "spill over" into all areas of your relationship.

SAMPLE "TURN ON" LIST

scuba diving
cooking

skiing
sex
massage
listening to good music
dancing
ice cream
being with good friends
working out

6. Periodically update your list. You may or may not want to include time spent on each activity.

7. It might be fun to decorate or artistically embellish your "turn on" list. Consider writing on colored paper with colored pens, sparkles, stickers, pictures, etc.

8. Make a collage of these activities from pictures found in magazines.

The practices in this chapter can help you focus more toward your feelings and your fun, if you'll let them. **Consider emphasizing these two practices in your life for at least two weeks before going on to the next chapter.** The goal is to incorporate these ideas and actions into your everyday life.

8

Balancing Our Lives for Health and Joy

We are all faced with an intense competition for our time. We must put in many hours at work, devote time to the children, maintain the home, attend social activities, create alone time and time with partners. Sometimes after a hard day's work, the thought of intimate communication or sex with our partner can be overwhelming.

Sally and Bill have been married ten years. They have two children and a dog. They live an upper middle-class lifestyle, maintained with two careers. Bill travels at least ten days out of every month. Sally commutes one hour each way to work. They have recently begun to question their love for each other. Sex has become infrequent and perfunctory. They came into couples therapy questioning the validity of their relationship. Both admitted that sex was hot and frequent early in their relationship but aren't sure what happened.

As the demands for their time increased, they have given less attention to each other. They yearn for the good old days early in their relationship when they felt so much in love and the passion ran hot. Why is it so different now? More importantly, how can they change it?

Perhaps you can remember during your courtship that your partner was your most important priority. Somehow you managed to find time to have extended lunches, take long walks, pass long hours in front of the fireplace with each other, or travel to romantic fun-filled places. Your thoughts were never very far from your love. You *can* feel that way again.

We can't do it all.

We are all besieged with demands for our precious time. Our job, our relatives, our kids, etc. Each of us could go thirty-six hours a day trying to do it all. We can't do it all. We have to decide what is most important in our life and then devote our time and attention. If your intimate relationship is most important, it must be put in the number 1 position.

Learning to balance your life as you *want* it means more balance for things which make you feel good. The first step to a more balanced lifestyle is to create adequate time to re-focus and pay attention to each other. It's important to set aside regular times that each partner can count on: to reconnect, to share feelings, to play, and to be understood.

This time for intimate and emotional connection is essential to build a strong foundation for good sex to flow. By committing to this time, you are communicating to each other that you are still number one in the other's lives.

Evaluating the ways you currently spend your time will provide an opportunity for you to consider whether or not you need to change the way you spend your time. More than likely, you will find it necessary to re-prioritize some activities in order to make more time for your relationship.

Practice

Purpose: Evaluating the ways you currently spend your time will provide an opportunity to change. After completing this exercise, you may wish to re-prioritize some activities in order to make more time for your relationship.

HOW DO YOU SPEND TIME?

1. Each partner is to record time spent each day by activity in 15-minute increments on a separate piece of paper.
2. Use slash marks if you wish.
3. Insert daily totals for each activity in charts below.
4. Look at totals for each category and rank by total amount of time spent, e.g., llll (1 hour 15 minutes)

NOTE: This exercise may appear onerous. Yes, it will take time, but it is invaluable. Please do NOT skip it. The results will be surprising, if not alarming.

PARTNER #1

	DAILY TOTALS							RANK BY TOTAL TIME	
	M	T	W	TH	F	S	S	Total	Rank
Sleep									
Eat/Food Preparation									
Work									
Commute/Travel									
TV									
Children/Family									
Shopping									
Alone Time									
Friends									
Entertainment									
Quality Time with Partner									
Sexual Time with Partner									
Exercise									
Other									
Other									

PARTNER #2

| | DAILY TOTALS ||||||| RANK BY TOTAL TIME ||
	M	T	W	TH	F	S	S	Total	Rank
Sleep									
Eat/Food Preparation									
Work									
Commute/Travel									
TV									
Children/Family									
Shopping									
Alone Time									
Friends									
Entertainment									
Quality Time with Partner									
Sexual Time with Partner									
Exercise									
Other									
Other									

Questions for each of you to answer upon completion of exercise:

- Are you spending your time the way you want?
- What areas are out of balance?
- Too much?
- Too little?
- How do you want to change the balance you see?
- What are you going to give up?

1. In what ways can each of you make adjustments so your schedule more accurately reflects your importance to each other?
2. Discuss the details of your findings with your partner and negotiate changes you want that will increase your intimate time together.
3. This idea of making your relationship and your sexual life more important takes commitment and effort. Be patient with yourself and with your partner.

The thirty minutes after a partner gets home from work is a time of emotional vulnerability and is ripe for conflict. Most couples find it is very helpful to have "decompression time." For some couples, this may mean spending 15-30 minutes alone, changing clothes, showering, listening to music, and then getting together. Others may want to sit down together as soon as they get home and check-in with one another. Sometimes you may want to schedule a "talk" time later in the evening. What is your style? What works best for you? Remember, the goal is to be totally present and relaxed for you and your partner.

Anyway you and your partner work it out, it is very important for loving couples to spend 15-30 minutes being with one another and communicating on a daily basis.

Anyway you and your partner work it out, it is very important for loving couples to spend 15-30 minutes being with one another and communicating on a daily basis.

With the rapid pace of our work-a-day world, it may seem as though there is little time to focus on our partner. By creating balance in your life and giving a greater priority to your total relationship, you will most likely find your sexual play will improve. It is also quite likely your overall health will improve. (See Chapter 14 on Health.)

After using the practice to examine the ways they were spending their time, Sally and Bill could more easily see how their attention had shifted away from their intimate relationship. With the help of this practice, Sally and Bill decided to change the focus of their daily lives. Bill decided to look for a job which demanded less travel. Sally began to telecommute one day a week. Her long-term goal is to be home three days a week. In addition, they committed to finding a regular babysitter and going out with each other on a date every Thursday. This last decision made each of them very happy. They were giggling when they left my office.

Challenge your beliefs about the work-play ratio in your life.

Challenge your beliefs about the work-play ratio in your life. **You *can* play before all your work is done!** You will come to believe you can be successful without more and more money. It may be difficult to modify your work ethic, but you will be pleasantly delighted. It will be worth it when your life is filled with fun, love, great sex and less feelings of pressure, and a heck of a lot more laughter.

Throughout this manual, there will be more tips on ways to bring increased balance into your life as you rekindle the passion for each other and gain new appreciation for the wonders of an intimate relationship. Balance brings increased energy, motivation, and productivity.

9

Self-Esteem and Body Image

Your self-image is the way you see yourself. Your self-image is demonstrated in the way you feel and act. It is also reflected in the people you bring into your life. If you think well of yourself, you will have vibrant, confident, mature, fun-loving people in your life, those who are much like you.

The image you have of your physical self, i.e., your body, is continuously reinforced by your expectations and perceptions. **You are truly who you think you are.**

If you **believe** you are attractive and sexy, you will tend to behave that way, and others will respond to you as if you are attractive and sexy. Regardless of an objective observer's evaluation, if you believe you are unattractive in any way, you will find that others will respond to you in ways other than you might want.

The way you see yourself and your body can profoundly affect your sexual responses. Your self-esteem plays an important role in determining your body image (and vice versa) and the ways you hold your body. For example, I often see women who believe they are too fat and not sexy enough. They refuse to wear attractive clothing, take care of their general appearance, and are afraid to be

Self-Esteem and Body Image • 73

naked with their spouse. They may be fearful of disapproval, but usually it is from themselves, not their partner. Needless to say, this reduces the amount of sexual contact between partners. In these kinds of situations, the husband often feels his wife is attractive and cannot understand her perceptions of herself. If you are one of these individuals, counseling may be indicated. How we see ourselves can be deeply imbedded in our ways of looking at the world, but this can be changed.

The next practice will help you understand some of the ways your feelings and judgments about your body may be reflected in your sexuality.

Practice

GETTING TO KNOW YOUR BODY

Purpose: Clarify feelings and image issues that might be affecting your sexuality.

1. Sit directly in front of your partner.
2. Be sure to listen and acknowledge your partner's feelings.
3. Be careful not to discount or challenge your partner's feelings. Feelings are just feelings.
4. Take turns answering the following questions:

   NOTE: If you are extremely self-conscious, do this exercise alone in front of a mirror first, and then do it in front of your spouse/partner.

   a. Three characteristics I like about my body are:

   _____

   _____

   _____

b. Three characteristics I don't like about my body are:

_____

_____

_____

c. One way I think my feelings about my body might diminish or decrease my sexual desire is:

_____

d. One way I think my feelings about my body might enhance or increase my sexual desire is:

_____

The next practice (Power of Affirmation) can be used to help you change your body image and subsequently your feelings about yourself. More about self-esteem first.

Although Lori is very attractive and personable, she has had great difficulty believing that her beauty is real. She used to shun strokes and was often the first one to put herself down. As a result of her poor self-image and low self-esteem, Lori consistently made poor choices about the men in her life. She was choosing men who did not like women but were drawn to attractive women. Lori came to therapy discouraged with pervasive, self-deprecating thoughts. She had just ended a four-year relationship and felt very emotionally battered. With hard work, much determination, and an emphasis on changing her thoughts with affirmations, she began to value herself more. As her self-esteem improved, she is moving away from old, destructive patterns in relationships, because she sees herself differently, both physically and sexually. Her thoughts about herself are more positive and self-nurturing with each passing day. She is finding joy in relationships with women as well as men, because her self-worth is no longer tied to the man in her life.

SELF-ESTEEM

Whether you call it self-respect, self-confidence or self-esteem, this concept refers to how much you, as an individual, value yourself. The ways in which you value yourself will have broad implications for the ways you treat yourself and your partner.

Although it is an old cliché, there is a ring of truth to: "You can't really love someone else until you love yourself." How you think about and value yourself will reflect and be reflected in the way you think about and value your partner. Those who often put their partner down, or nag continuously, usually do not feel very good about themselves.

Your self-esteem is directly related to the thoughts you have about yourself. If you are always criticizing yourself and putting yourself down in one way or another, it will be impossible to think well of yourself and feel optimistic. Likewise, if you believe you should not or could not change, you may be hampering the positive evolution of your sexual relationship. Beliefs and thoughts are interrelated and dominate our lives and our choices.

Thoughts reflect beliefs and feelings. Thoughts also direct feelings and beliefs. By changing your thoughts you can change your feelings and your behaviors. Affirmations can be used to modify and improve your thoughts about you, your life, and your sexuality.

**By changing your thoughts
you can change your feelings and your behaviors.**

Maybe your self-image has prevented you from feeling better about your sexuality. You can change those thoughts as well as the behaviors which are hindering you in having the relationship of your dreams. Acting and thinking confidently can bring greater feelings of well-being and self-confidence.

Practice

POWER OF AFFIRMATION

Purpose: To create new ways of thinking, feeling, and being.

Set aside 30 minutes with your self.

An Affirmation is a positive statement of truth or that which you desire to be true.

1. Create a thought you *want* to have about

    a. Your self-image

    b. Your sexuality

    c. Your partner

    d. Your relationship

    You might like to start with a thought that is almost true or mostly true, until you get more confidence about the power of affirmations.

2. Use the following steps to complete your affirmation.

    a. Write it down (writing something down enhances learning and makes it more real)

    b. State in the positive. Avoid use of don't, won't, or not.

    c. Be succinct, e.g., *I love my shoulders*

    d. Be specific, e.g., *my sexual interest is increasing*

    e. Make it magnetic and attractive to you, e.g., *I am excited when I think about my partner, wife or husband. I am falling in love all over again.*

    f. State it as if it already exists. Use present time, e.g., *I'm feeling more sensitivity and pleasure in my body.*

    g. Keep it personal: Use "I" or "my"

h. Focus on your thoughts only, not on the thoughts of others.

i. Change affirmations regularly to avoid boredom and to push your own limits of change.

j. To incorporate your affirmations to most enrich your life

   (1) Read them 10-20 times a day

   (2) Recite them out loud twice a day

   (3) Rewrite them one time a day

We believe that feeling sexy and easily aroused is a complex system of beliefs about sex, femininity, bodies, and pleasure.

Continuing with the use of affirmations, the following mini-practices address the frequently described feelings of not liking your body "enough." Women often believe that their body is not attractive enough. Sometimes they think they would feel more sexy or aroused if their body was more beautiful. We believe that feeling sexy and easily aroused is a complex system of beliefs about sex, femininity, bodies, and pleasure. Having these beliefs in line with what you want provides the foundation for a fully sexual woman. You may have the body of a movie star, but a lack of love and appreciation of your body and your self-worth may be obstacles to feeling fully sexual and happy with yourself.

These comments are equally true for a man, even though it is not as common for a man to feel this way as a woman. Men who are confused about their worth in this world of changing values often suffer a diminished interest in sex, and much of it is related to low self-esteem.

MINI-PRACTICE

A. Although this practice may feel as if it is for the female partner, it is appropriate for both sexes. Sit in front of a mirror and tell yourself out loud, "*I am sexy. I am attractive. It is okay for me to feel sexy. It is wonderful for me to act sexy. In my heart I know I am a sexual person. My body is learning what it means to be a sexual woman/man. As I learn more and more about my body and my sensations, I am becoming more comfortable with and enthusiastic about my sexuality."* Repeat these thoughts three times at each daily sitting. Say them out loud at least once a day. Although this sounds like a simple exercise, the power of affirmation can change your life. Please feel free to change the specific wording to that which fits you best.

B. Look at the **Body Image Practice** at the beginning of this chapter. Take each of the three characteristics you do like and the three characteristics you don't like about your body. Using the guidelines in the Power of Affirmative Practice, create six affirmations incorporating these six characteristics. You will have three positive and three you will have to change to positive. Repeat these affirmations 10-20 times a day.

You are truly who you think you are.

Section 2

Sex, Love and You

10

Gender Differences: Yes, Virginia, Men and Women Come from Different Planets

The differences between boys and girls are observable very early in life. Little girls learn to talk, on the average, earlier than little boys. Girls practice their verbal skills at a greater rate and talk more about feelings and emotional reactions than do boys. Boys learn to act and do, with much less talk and introspection than girls. These differences are socially accepted and promoted, and usually continue into adulthood. **You can't grow up in this society without confused sexual messages being a part of who you are.**

Women, in general, are more comfortable than men with emotional intimacy and talking about feelings. In contrast, men are usually more accepting of their sexuality and feel more comfortable thinking, and perhaps talking about sex.

Women learn to turn off sexual feelings and impulses early in life because openness about sexuality is not "okay" for a female in our society. Segments of our culture teach that genitals are dirty and sex is immoral. As a result of the discomfort generated about sex, romance becomes the focus of a woman's attention instead of explicit sexuality.

In contrast, men in our society are given much greater liberty to think about, fantasize about, and act upon their sexual impulses. While it is usually the woman who initiates emotionally intimate verbal communication, recent surveys suggest it is still the man who initiates sexual activity 65% of the time. Women trade sex for love and intimacy, whereas men trade love and intimacy for sex.

As women experience and accept their sexuality more fully, and men take more responsibility for their feelings, these differences will diminish, creating a much more sex-positive culture.

Overcoming early gender role training is desireable for a couple to be fully sexual and intimate. It begins with awareness and then consciousness. Reading about sex-role differences and understanding the influences of your family of origin can be a great first step. It is important to have an ongoing dialogue with your partner about modifications you would like to have in your relationship on all levels.

Women trade sex for love and intimacy, whereas men trade love and intimacy for sex.

Practice

GENDER ROLE

It is important to recognize that many issues of conflict are gender related, some learned, some perhaps biologically based. In addition to learning more about your selves, this exercise can help each of you to identify more clearly those issues that are gender generated rather than partner (lover) generated.

Set aside an hour to do this practice.

- List below and then share with your partner at least five (5) beliefs you have about men and women. Include feelings, attitudes, interests, reactions, physical issues, sexuality, personality, e.g., *"Men want sex more than women." "Men don't need foreplay like women do." "Men love sports." "Women are too sensitive." "Men are not attracted to women who are too smart."*

Partner #1 List

_____
_____
_____
_____
_____

Partner #2 List

_____
_____
_____
_____
_____

- After you have completed the above lists, partner 1 state your first belief; listen as your partner describes his or her reactions to your belief. Do this with each belief. Listen only to understand, not for agreement. No arguing. The goal is to learn about yourself and your partner, not who is right or wrong.
- Reverse roles as described above, i.e., speaker becomes listener.
- Some gender differences (communication style, energy level, job description, dependence on feelings, etc.) can interfere with emotional intimacy in a loving relationship. Examine with your

partner the gender differences you think and/or feel may be interfering with your feelings of closeness and intimacy.[1]

- **Check gender differences that may be interfering with intimacy in your relationship.**

Partner A	Partner B	
_____	_____	Work is too important
_____	_____	Kids are too important
_____	_____	Sex is too important
_____	_____	Sex isn't important enough
_____	_____	He never talks to me
_____	_____	She always nags
_____	_____	He/she never listens
_____	_____	He only thinks about his needs
_____	_____	There's no touching without him wanting sex
_____	_____	He always wants sex after an argument
_____	_____	She is not okay with masturbation
_____	_____	He/she doesn't want to talk about sex
_____	_____	He likes (she doesn't) sexually explicit videos
_____	_____	He never shares his feelings
_____	_____	He wants me to stop everything I'm doing for sex
_____	_____	Men have fragile egos
_____	_____	Oral sex is unclean
_____	_____	He/she doesn't initiate sex enough

---

[1] Bibliography in Appendix lists books which address subject of gender differences and ways to deal with them.

- **List any additional beliefs, attitudes, or behaviors that could be obstacles in your relationship that are based in gender differences.**

  _____

  _____

  _____

- **List below *one way* that each of you can behave in a new way, for each gender difference that is an obstacle you have listed above.**

His List	Her List
_____	_____
_____	_____
_____	_____
_____	_____
_____	_____

For example, many women complain that men raise their voices, and it feels as if the man is angry. When she believes he is angry, she either gets very defensive and angry in return or withdraws. This appears to be based on culturally bound responses. *One thing that the man might do is consciously speak more softly. One thing the woman could do is gently let the man know, without judgment, that she is responding negatively and has a desire to withdraw.* It is important that both the man and the woman think of at least one way to behave differently for each obstacle noted.

DOUBLE STANDARDS

Throughout history and in most cultures today, sexual double standards for the male and the female have affected the type and quality of the sexuality available. Traditionally, a male child receives a form of approval for "sowing his wild oats." Losing his virginity is a rite of passage into adulthood for a young male. For a young woman, it is still something that is "taken from her," and she is often too embarrassed to talk about sex.

In many cultures, a man having a mistress is tolerated, sometimes esteemed. However, a woman will be ostracized or punished for having a lover. A married woman is "supposed" to be tolerant of her man's affair. A married man is considered "wronged" if his wife has an affair. A man is less likely to forgive and will more often leave his relationship in the event of an affair by his wife than will a woman.

Some men are very uncomfortable when a woman initiates any kind of sexual activity. His cultural mores indicate that only he is to make the first move. This perspective is prevalent in the dating scene where a woman holds back and hopes the man of her choice will notice her.

Similarly, a wife has been expected to be sexually available when the husband wants sex. It has been considered her "wifely duty." It is not relevant whether or not she enjoys the sexual encounter. Historically, sex has been on his timetable, not hers.

When John and Elissa came for counseling, the primary complaint was that John thought Elissa was turned off to him because she never let him know when she wanted to be sexual.

Elissa's upbringing prohibited her from being sexually explicit. She had learned that it was not ladylike to ask for sex. However, John believed that if she loved him, she would desire to be sexual. He felt not desired as a man when she didn't let him know of her sexual desires. With counseling, Elissa worked through the messages she received from her mother. Her mother had taught her by example as well as by explicit words and threats.

Elissa's mother was raised in a fundamentalist religious household in which sex was viewed only as a means of procreation and certainly not for pleasure, especially a woman's pleasure. There were many ways of being sexual that felt good to Elissa, but she felt guilty and betrayed by her body enjoying these baser instincts.

John had a normal, healthy sex drive for a man his age but began to feel that he wasn't sexually desired by Elissa and that perhaps he was abnormally sexual.

With support and encouragement in counseling, Elissa started to acknowledge her sexual feelings as okay and healthy. John learned new techniques that helped him slow down and make it safer and more comfortable for Elissa to feel his touch with greater pleasure.

John learned to recognize other ways Elissa showed him love besides sex. His feelings for Elissa deepened as he felt more expression from Elissa. Gradually, Elissa began to let him know more openly about her sexual desires, as she felt more comfortable with her own sexuality and more approving of John's sexual desires.

In our practice, we often encounter the female who is assertive in many arenas of her life but never initiates sexual play. Double standards frequently can result in feelings of inequality. **Anger and resentment can result from these unspoken double standards that construct psychological walls preventing greater emotional and sexual intimacy.**

There are many common double standards which influence our sexuality. Because these standards are often preconscious, we may act on them without being aware they exist. Similarly we can believe that our partner holds the same beliefs when nothing could be further from the truth

The following practice can assist you in bringing these double standards to the conscious level.

MINI-PRACTICE

- Please discuss with your partner the double standards which you perceive to be currently active in your sexual relationship, i.e., what's okay for one of you, but not the other.

- In what ways would each of you like to see each of these modified?

- What is one thing (attitude or behavior) you would be willing to do differently to begin to change the double standards in your sexual relationship?

11

Anger and Sex Make Terrible Bed Partners

In order for you to have satisfying and playful sex, all angers that either of you hold must be addressed. When you are angry or holding a resentment, there is a part of you that is not available to enjoy the closeness and playfulness that is necessary for satisfying sexual experience.

ORIGINS OF ANGER

Anger has its origin in the "fight or flight syndrome" of mammals. The organism (you) gets aroused (agitated) when it feels threatened or not in control. This is the so-called "reptilian brain" that is stimulated.

Anger may be described as a sense of powerlessness, a feeling you cannot control a person, situation, or the environment. Have you noticed that you rarely get angry when you have a sense of control of the events in your life?

Anger does not give anyone license to batter a partner emotionally or physically. Anger usually comes from deep inside, from some place early in childhood when something was wanted and denied.

Those who get the angriest are usually those who have been the most deprived of love, affection, approval, and acceptance.

**Those who get the angriest
are usually those who have been the most deprived
of love, affection, approval, and acceptance.**

When you are enraged, it is impossible to think clearly. Intense emotions overwhelm your logical mind and your small, hurt, inner child lashes out. This is not the time to talk or try to solve a problem.

Maybe you associate violence with anger. Perhaps you feel that love is being taken away when your partner gets angry. There are many reasons why someone feels anger is "bad" and something to be feared and avoided. Most of us have not been taught how to express anger in ways that feel safe and non-abusive, nor have we been taught to be in the presence of another's anger without feeling we have to take responsibility for it.

When we were children, we had no way of evaluating the appropriateness of the anger we were feeling from grown-ups around us. As you grow into adulthood, you may withdraw, blame, shout, hit, pout, or plan some revenge, because you learned those behaviors as a child. Your anger often feels as if it is the responsibility of your partner or another person in your world. You may say, "You made me mad." When you are angry, you not only want to blame the other person; you may want to hurt or lash out at the other person, emotionally or physically.

OWNING YOUR ANGER

To effectively deal with your anger, it is essential to first accept it as a normal human emotion and take sole responsibility for your anger. Once you deeply believe that your anger is solely your own, and therefore only you can do anything about it, you can move beyond the anger and more freely choose a loving and productive way to approach your partner.

Melanie and Greg came in for counseling because they were always arguing, and the slightest discussion quickly turned into anger. When the last conflict resulted in Greg grabbing Melanie and pushing her across the room, both decided they needed help.

In the first session, it was easy to see that neither Melanie nor Greg owned their own feelings, thoughts, and responses. They proceeded to blame one another and throw sarcastic barbs. Their language was filled with many "you" (blaming or attacking) statements rather than "I" (owning) statements.

The therapist quickly took charge and made it clear that blaming one another would only lead to further hard feelings, escalation of anger, and greater emotional distance between them. This step of owning one's anger is closely related to maturing as an adult—moving past the fear of a child's anger and power, and believing that you are the only one in charge of you.

When we take full responsibility for our feelings, thoughts, and behaviors, we are taking control of our lives.

When we take full responsibility for our feelings, thoughts, and behaviors, we are taking control of our lives. Our society tends to teach "passing the buck." **If I'm feeling angry (or sad or happy), it must be someone else's fault. Well, it isn't.** You, alone, are the creator, generator of your reactions, both emotional and physical. Only you can do something about it.

When you give the responsibility for your feelings to another, you are giving away your power. You will never have control over your partner's feelings and reactions. If you fixate on your need to have your partner change in order for you to be okay, you will continuously be in a powerless position, regardless of your argumentative stance.

It was made clear to Melanie and Greg that no blaming or fault-finding would be tolerated. They would be asked to cease their blaming tactics and look inward to their individual feelings beneath the anger. Anger never comes alone; it is merely a signal to look deeper. Anger is most frequently a cover for feelings of helplessness, frustration, or powerlessness.

Anger is most frequently a cover for feelings of helplessness, frustration, or powerlessness.

Learning to face one's feelings and to let go of the defense of blaming someone else requires close attention, a trusted friend (and/or lover) to call you on it, and a willingness to change your approach to life. Affirmations can also be helpful in changing your thinking, e.g., *I'm changing my old patterns. I am learning to take responsibility for me. I'm in charge of my life. I can use my anger to look inward. I'm not responsible for my partner's reactions. I'm responsible for mine.*

Melanie and Greg began to understand that anger is a response of personal powerlessness. As each tried to control the other person's opinions or behaviors, each person was giving up her/his own personal power to the other. Their use of "you" further armed each to a defensive position. There was no way each could understand the other's feelings or behaviors while feeling under attack and blamed.

In subsequent sessions, Greg and Melanie learned to use "I" messages rather than "you" and believe them. They discovered that when they used "I," the listener was more able to hear what the speaker was saying since the listener didn't feel attacked. They were taught the "No Response Technique." This helped them feel emotionally safer in delivering communications to each other. They were also surprised to learn how much more they heard as the listener, when they didn't have the need to prepare a defense for their partner's attack.

Another technique Melanie and Greg learned to further take responsibility for their own anger was the *time out technique*, which is explained later in this chapter. Both agreed that they appreciated the "break" to let their feelings settle down and their heads clear enough to more rationally consider each other's wants and points of view.

A resentment can be thought of as a "premature" anger or an unexpressed anger. Resentment is often lurking inside and waiting for just the right moment to come out to punish your partner. You

92 • *Intimacy*

often fail to express the little angers and resentments (i.e., stuff them), believing that they are insignificant, or desiring not to "rock the boat." These withheld angers do not go away. When you have "stuffed" to your limit, you explode with the next provocation, however minor.

Anger can be a relationship problem when it is either withheld, as described above, or expressed explosively and unpredictably.

THREE STEPS OF THE **TIME OUT**

A good tool to use when anger is escalating is a "time out." A time-out process must be understood and agreed upon during a time of talking about problems and negotiating mutual agreements around them. This discussion is done at a time other than during an argument.

The three steps of the time out are:

1. One partner indicates need for a break by saying "time out," which stops an angry interaction.

2. Both agree to a time for getting back together to talk (this step is critical for mutual reassurance that neither partner is going to feel abandoned).

3. Keep the time agreement. If you are still feeling angry, renegotiate a new time agreement. This maintains a feeling of trust and integrity between partners as you strive to resolve your conflict. Do not change the time agreement more than twice.

STEPS FOR COPING WITH ANGER

The following steps can be helpful for dealing with your anger.

Pre-Time Out

1. Be aware of your anger. Watch for signs, e.g., tightness in chest or jaw, sweating palms, stomach ache, rapid breathing, desire to run away or go in your cave, etc.

During Time Out

2. Own your anger. It's your anger. Your partner did not make you angry; you allowed yourself to get angry. You have a button that got pushed. It's important not to blame. Blaming places you in a helpless situation.

3. Deal with the physical part of your anger until you feel your system calm down (exercise, scream into a pillow, go for a walk, etc.). This varies from a few minutes to a day or two. The longer you hang onto it, the deeper the wounding that needs to be addressed.

4. Ask yourself, what part of you reacted angrily in this situation? (Which of your emotional buttons got pushed? What are you feeling powerless about? You didn't get your way about what? What about your control?)

5. What do you *really* want from your partner? (Reassurance, understanding, support, affection, love, etc.)

6. How are you going to ask for what you really want? (tone of voice, "I" messages, no blaming or criticizing)

Post Time Out

7. Communicate feelings, needs, and wants to partner in an honest, open, and non-blaming manner.

The two hardest but most fundamental things to learn in a relationship come into focus with anger:

1. How to take complete and total responsibility for your feelings and actions;

2. How to approach your partner in a way that will facilitate growth and change rather than defensiveness and closing down.

Practice

"CLEARING THE DECKS FOR GOOD SEX"

This is a tool you can use to "clear the decks" of any unspoken angers or withheld communications.

Before you can put yourself in a space of intimacy and vulnerability with your partner, it's important that you are feeling a sense of closeness and good will toward each other. If either partner is holding onto angers, irritations, or unfinished business, the quality of your sexual experience will surely be diminished.

- **Face each other in straight-back chairs, making eye contact with each other, and touching knees.**
- **Gently hold each other's hands.**
- **One partner will begin by requesting of the other, "Tell me something you have withheld from me."**
- **The responding partner communicates any feeling or emotion that may help him or her "clear their deck" (mind), so he/she can feel closer to his/her partner. Be sure to use an "I" message, i.e., you describe only your feeling or thought.**
    - It can be a negative withhold such as, "I felt angry at you yesterday. You didn't take out the garbage after you said you would."
    - It can be a positive withhold such as, "I forgot to tell you how much I appreciated you taking the kids off my hands last Tuesday."
    - Each person gets 10 minutes to "clear the decks."
- **There is to be no response from the listening partner, except a "thank you" and "tell me something you've withheld from me." The purpose is to get the feelings out, release the energy, *not* to fix or change anything.**

- **At the end of the 10 minutes, switch to let the other partner clear the decks.**

Initially this can be a scary practice. It is practice for both the speaker and the listener. The speaker must learn to face his/her fear of retaliation and being blamed, while the listener must face her/his fear of being blamed, wronged, and unloved.

Remember that your overall goal is one of being a full human being who loves yourself. Facing your fears and moving through them is a profound step in that direction. When you truly love yourself, you will be open to the love and humanness of another, i.e., your partner.

12

Love and Affection

When asked, "what is love?," each of us would have a unique response. By the time you reach your twenties, you have probably "fallen in love" at least once. There is little difference between falling in love and infatuation. Infatuation is the state one experiences when a new person comes into your life. It feels so passionate and exciting. This is a process of discovery and validation for the best you are and can be. It is a period of time when both physical and verbal stroking levels are great. It is a time of emotional highs, tenderness, and sexuality. It is as though you cannot get enough of the other person. Your lover is on your mind a great part of the waking day.

This kind of love is such an emotional high we want it to go on forever. Some individuals believe they are no longer "in love" when those intense, hot feelings begin to subside. Is love really dead, or is love, perhaps, an ever-changing, ever-evolving emotion?

Judith Viorst defined the difference between infatuation, i.e., falling in love, and being in love:

> *"Infatuation is when you think that he is as sexy as Robert Redford, as smart as Henry Kissinger, as noble as Ralph Nader, as funny as Woody Allen, and as athletic as Jimmy Connors. Love is when you realize he is as sexy as Woody Allen, as smart as Jimmy Connors, as funny as Ralph Nader, as athletic as Henry Kissinger, and nothing like Robert Redford in any category—but you will take him anyway."*

Affection is love growing in all aspects. It encompasses a deepening friendship and understanding of your partner. It is an appreciation and acceptance of the negative as well as the positive aspects of each other. It is a feeling of goodwill and friendship. It is a feeling of warmth, tenderness, and playfulness.

There is a pride in the history and depth that you have created and are creating with each other. Our professional experience has led us to believe that the most overwhelming factor contributing to longevity of a relationship is the feeling (and the thought), "this is my best friend."

Loving is a process, not an end state. The hows and ways you relate to one another are fundamental in building the bonds of the future. In the courtship phase of a relationship, a key feature is the feeling of importance to the other. You know you are wanted and valued in your partner's life. To recapture and maintain some of those great emotional highs, you must give your partner the time and attention commensurate with those early days. You must focus on your partner with the attention it takes to spark these loving feelings.

The most overwhelming factor contributing to longevity of a relationship is the feeling (and the thought), "this is my best friend."

Terry and Donna are an attractive couple in their late thirties. They have two great kids and live comfortably. Donna works part-time and is home when the kids arrive from school. Terry and Donna came for counseling to explore why they felt distant from each other emotionally and were having sex only once or twice a month. Donna, in a dejected tone: "It feels as though we've slowly fallen out of love with other."

Both admitted that after their children were born, the amount of time they took for themselves was minimal. Even their vacation time for the last two years was spent at home. They seemed to be handling the "logistics" of their marriage well. They had become good "business partners" while slowly and subtly letting their loving emotions for each other die.

Both agreed their courtship had been romantic and fun-filled. They were deeply in love with each other when they were married seven years ago. Now, it had been months since they had gone out on a "date" with each other without the kids.

In counseling, Terry and Donna learned that they could rekindle their courtship feelings by using several ideas discussed in this book. This chapter helped them recall the many behaviors each did for the other that made them feel loved during their courtship. They examined their allocation of time with the help of the chart in Chapter 8.

Terry admitted that they probably wouldn't have had a courtship at all if they had allocated their time then the way they were doing it now.

Within weeks, Donna acknowledged that she felt loving feelings returning for Terry as he gave her the kind of attention that assured her that she was the important priority in his life. She started to feel beautiful and sexy again. Terry also noticed that Donna was responding to him with more acknowledgments and affection. He no longer felt he was only appreciated for the paychecks he brought home.

Practice

Purpose: Using memories of your courtship, you and your partner can gain new perspectives on the behaviors that prompted each of you to feel loved by the other.

FALLING IN LOVE, AGAIN

- **Sitting with your partner, take turns reminiscing about your early courtship and "Being in Love."**
- **Breathe deeply, letting go of walls.**

1. What was your favorite date?

2. When did you know you were in love?

3. What one thing did your partner do or say that expressed her/his love more dearly to you?

4. What was the most romantic experience you shared during courtship? Ever?

5. What was the most playful/exciting experience of your courtship?

6. Anything else about your courtship you would like to tell your partner.

Although we each say we want to love and be loved, most are afraid of not getting the love we want. **As with all of life, one must take risks to really feel loved.** Some of Donna's "shut down" of love feelings came as a result of her fear she couldn't be loved if she were honest and open. This playbook is about facing yourself, your fears, and your human qualities, and allowing yourself to be loved, regardless of imperfections.

Practice

GIVING AND RECEIVING LOVE

Purpose: To give each of you practice in asking for what you want, negotiating, making agreements. Very importantly, it is to provide you with daily opportunities to express and receive loving and affectionate behaviors.

- Take turns asking your partner, "What is one thing I can do or say differently that would feel loving and affectionate to you if I did it regularly? (Be specific.) Keep the requests small and observable.

Do this until you have created a list of five behaviors for each of you.

EXAMPLES (REMEMBER TO BE PLAYFUL)

1. A kiss and/or hug good-bye in AM.
2. Wake me up with a kiss in AM.
3. Turn off TV and talk about your day—10-20 minutes every day.
4. Compliment or acknowledgment at least once a day.
5. A five-minute neck rub.

- **Create a chart for each of you with each behavior followed by seven squares denoting the days of the week, beginning with the current day.**
- **Mark off for each day when your partner has completed his/her behavior. It is the receiver who marks it, not the giver.**
- **After seven days, sit down and discuss how you feel about the behaviors and each other.**
- **You will probably wish to continue most of the behaviors because they feel so good. Modify as needed for loving feelings.**

Many people think falling in love is the start of the relationship. We believe that love is the ongoing process that results when all the components we have discussed in this chapter are practiced within an intimate relationship. Emotional intimacy including feeling loved and important allows you to open to the possibility of ever deepening levels of physical intimacy. **Emotional intimacy is the green light for red hot sex!**

13

Romance to Warm Up Your Nights and Days

Women want romance and men want sex. Is that not the classic line? Why is it most men have such difficulty understanding what romance means to a woman and the important role it plays in her life? Why do many women believe that all men want is sex, and this thought turns them off? Without trying to describe all the differences between men and women in this short chapter, suffice it to say that men and women perceive love and sexuality differently for a wide variety of reasons. (See Chapter 10 for some of the reasons.)

Romance is the language of love. Romance communicates to a woman that she is special in her man's eyes and heart. Men are hesitant to act romantically because of a lack of certainty as to what a woman thinks romance to be. They may also think romance is non-manly or that he simply cannot be that way.

It may be difficult for the woman to explain what romance is. She may believe that if she has to explain it or ask for romance, it is diminished or somehow does not count.

ROMANCE IS:

1. *Giving* your partner undivided attention;

2. *Communicating* your intimate feelings of love for her (or him);
3. *Considering* your partner's needs and desires.
4. *Listening* and inquiring to ensure your partner feels cared about;
5. *Demonstrating* your desire for your partner;
6. *Showing* your partner that you love and consider her/him special;
7. *Letting your partner know* that you want him/her to feel loved and considered.
8. *Doing* the spontaneous, the surprising, the unpredictable.

Romance is often considered the domain of the woman. However, it is our experience that a majority of men enjoy romantic attention as well.

It is our experience that a majority of men enjoy romantic attention as well.

Romance is usually present in the courtship phase of a relationship. After marriage, many couples get distracted by careers, babies, making money, etc. As romantic gestures fade, feelings of being loved and cherished often wane.

This was the case with Ted and Alice. After seven years of marriage, two children and three moves, their courting behavior had essentially disappeared. Alice was on the verge of an affair with a co-worker with whom she felt important and cherished. Ted was in shock when he found out. He had assumed everything was just fine in the relationship.

After working through a great deal of anger and disappointment, both Ted and Alice agreed they wanted their marriage to not only last, but they wanted to feel more loving and sexy with one another. By looking at their courtship and the early days of their marriage, both were able to see how they had gradually made children and careers more of a priority than their relationship, as each partner had focused less loving attention on each other. Each acknowledged that they felt less loved and appreciated than earlier in their marriage.

As trust grew, the therapist was able to coach Alice in describing specifically what behaviors, tones, and words she desired from Ted. Alice remembered an endearing note Ted had sent soon after they had met. He had enclosed a love poem. Ted was surprised at the impact of that small gesture. He agreed to send Alice cards and notes with regular irregularity.

In similar fashion, Ted asked for a big smile from Alice, when they first met after a day's work. Ted always remembered feeling loved and very special when Alice smiled broadly at him. By continuing this process of focusing on the pleasurable details in their courtship, Alice and Ted identified eight behaviors that each used to do and wanted to resume with one another.

Practice

ROMANCE

Purpose: To identify romantic behaviors you might enjoy and to assist you in thinking romantically.

Below are some romantic behaviors. Each partner is to check off the ones which sound appealing. Please feel free to add your own. Discuss with your partner what you learn about yourself and your partner as you go through the practice.

____ ____ 1. Getting a babysitter and going to a local motel/hotel for the night.

____ ____ 2. Let the kids stay overnight at someone else's house and turn your bedroom into a getaway place.

____ ____ 3. Surprise your partner with a getaway to a local romantic spot for the weekend.

____ ____ 4. Send flowers and/or romantic cards.

____ ____ 5. Go on a hot-air balloon ride, glider ride, train ride, boat ride, etc. Surprise or not surprise.

____ ____ 6. Surprise night on the town, or plane trip.

____ ____ 7. Surprise night at the opera, theater, concert, with friends, etc.

____ ____ 8. Picnic. Surprise or not.

____ ____ 9. Surprise birthday party.

____ ____ 10. Return to the spot where you met, or had your first date or got married, etc.

____ ____ 11. Be affectionate in public.

____ ____ 12. Slow sensual massage.

____ ____ 13. An unexpected gift.

____ ____ 14. Write a love note or poem.

____ ____ 15. Have a special portrait made of you and give to your partner.

____ ____ 16. Call your partner on phone just to say I love you.

____ ____ 17. Holding hands while watching TV.

____ ____ 18. Go for a walk, alone together, every evening.

(fill in your own)

____ ____ _____

____ ____ _____

____ ____ _____

Use as many lines as you need. Use a separate piece of paper should you run out of space. The more ideas the better.

Make a personal commitment to make one of the above happen within one month. Remember to set the mood early. Plan to *try one new behavior each month.* You will be most pleasantly surprised with the results.

All romance is enhanced when positive, loving feelings are flowing between partners. Romance is fun for all, but usually requires a little (or a lot) of thought. Romance can add that extra spice necessary for not only great sex but great love. For many individuals it will not come naturally and will have to be learned and focused on.

Remember to say "I love you" often. Don't be stingy. You can't say "I love you" too much, unless you don't mean it.

Romance can add that extra spice necessary for not only great sex but great love.

FLIRTING

Another way to promote romantic fun is flirting. How long has it been since you flirted with your partner? Do you gaze at him playfully through half-closed eyelashes, or whisper seductive words in his ear? Do you bring her flowers and surprise her with a weekend getaway? Do you lower your voice and let her know what an attractive sexy woman she is?

Flirting for humans is similar to the courtship dances of many other species. The main purpose of flirting is to attract the attention of the opposite sex. Flirting is titillating and enticing. Flirting makes great use of sexual innuendo. Flirting involves all the senses: verbal, body language, touching, hearing, and smelling. Flirting is playful and often employs a good sense of humor. Flirting is a means of validation from the opposite sex, making you feel more attractive and desirable. When you're feeling attractive and desirable, you will be more eager to be intimate and sexual with your partner. After a long, hard day, flirting may help lighten the load, even if it doesn't end in sex play. It will, certainly, pave the way for deeper intimacy and sex at a better time. Incorporating flirtatious behavior in your relationship, you'll be ensuring a more exciting sex life, not to mention a heck of a lot more fun.

Practice

FLIRTING

Purpose: Each of you may be attracted by certain forms of flirting more than others. We've included the practice below to help clarify what kinds of flirting are more exciting and romantic for each partner.

Set aside 30 minutes to discuss with your partner the kind(s) of flirting you want more of. You can use this time to let your partner know about any flirting behavior(s) you would like your partner to change. Check off the types of flirting you particularly like. Use the rest of the time to be specific. Be sure you make this playful.

____ ____ 1. Verbal flirting (I love you, you're beautiful, I appreciate you, wow)

____ ____ 2. Visual flirting (dress, eyes, facial expression, etc.)

____ ____ 3. Body language

____ ____ 4. Touch (spontaneous gestures)

____ ____ 5. Sexual innuendo (seduction)

____ ____ 6. Smell (perfumes, colognes, etc.)

____ ____ 7. Humor

(fill in your own)

____ ____ 8. _____

____ ____ 9. _____

____ ____ 10. _____

Make a daily practice of flirting in the way(s) your partner has indicated he or she prefers. Flirting is a special form of communication that will add spice to your romantic and sexual relationship.

Keep in mind, this is the man/woman you fell in love with and want to be with for a long time. **Don't you want to stay juicy?**

TIMING

Timing is critical to the success of any sexual experience you may be planning. Timing is a function of listening and staying tuned into your partner. You may feel aroused or interested in sexual play. Before you make your move, it's in your best interest to check out your partner's mood. *Flirting is* a great way to check out your partner's openness to play. Many men prefer a direct inquiry often and believe that is what women want too. However, most women prefer a more subtle, indirect approach. Some women get turned off by a direct request. **Never assume your partner wants the same thing you do.** It is a sure way to not get what you want.

Be aware of other stressors that may take away from the mood you want to create. There might be something unexpected that comes up. In such a case, it's usually best to be flexible with the situation and alter your plans accordingly.

SEXUAL AGENDAS

You know you have a sexual agenda (rigid expectation) when you feel anger, disappointment, resentment and/or rejection when your partner doesn't respond positively to your romantic and sexual invitation. This applies even when a "date" with your partner has been set up beforehand.

Having a sexual agenda increases the chance one or both of you will feel victimized and unloved. Keep in mind that insisting on following through with your date (your agenda) will probably mean your partner won't be fully present to play. This will create anger and resentment in one or both of you. It is a set-up to lose.

Staying open to possibilities and being in the moment with your partner is a set-up to win. Looking for a setup to win means having the flexibility to "shift gears," i.e., to let go of your pleasurable plans for pleasure and not sink into anger and disappointment. A good way to approach this situation is to ask your partner and yourself, "If we can't make love, etc., what is the next most pleasurable or fun experience we can have?" This creates a dialogue of looking for that which both of you are willing or able to get excited about. This strategy can pave the way to your original desired activity to happen in the near future without putting yourself in the position of having to deal with anger, disappointment, and feelings of deprivation. *Let go of making sex a direct indicator of your partner's love.*

It's important for the man to know his partner's monthly cycle, since some people don't feel comfortable having sex play during menses. There are also certain times during each women's cycle that she feels more sexual. For some, it's at ovulation or just before menses. For others, it may be just after menses. This is useful information for both of you. If you don't know the answer, playfully measure the woman's interest in sex for a month or two.

Timing is essential when sexual play gets under way. It's important to go slowly and be sensitive to the level of your partner's arousal. (See Chapter 22 on Loveplay.) Your communication with each other during sex can aid in your awareness of your timing. For instance, you will know when to proceed as arousal increases or when to "back off" to delay orgasm.

SETTING THE MOOD

A good plan and a series of attractive invitations will start to peak your partner's interest.

Among the factors that enhance the quality of your sex life are good planning and an attractive invitation for the experience. These may begin hours, days, or even weeks before the actual sexual experience. Setting the mood includes anything that will help you feel excited and desirous for the actual experience. Taking the time to fantasize, i.e., think about, and plan for the utmost pleasure of each person can be exciting in itself.

By now, you have learned the importance of good communication to good sex and have learned a lot about your partner's turn-ons and turn-offs. Because of your increased awareness you are feeling more confident about creating a plan that will be pleasing and exciting to your partner. A good plan and a series of attractive invitations will start to peak your partner's interest. This is part of the process of extended "foreplay" or "loveplay."

Attractive invitations mean giving of yourself in special ways your partner will notice and appreciate. This can start with sexy notes, cards, flowers, flirting, or small gifts. It can be the way you dress, the scents you wear, the way you move, or a look. Sometimes thinking back to the courtship days will provide some valuable clues. Throughout this whole "dance," the main thing to remember is to keep your attention focused on your partner. This will let your partner know he/she is important to you. This importance will also be reflected by the amount of thought and planning you put into this special experience.

You are probably wondering if you have to do this every time you want to be sexual. If the two of you agree that spontaneous quickies are great, and each of you acknowledges and agrees to a way of initiating these encounters, please go for it. For many couples, the fun, the play, the romance, the thoughtfulness becomes an ongoing nurturing of desire. When this is the case, slipping into a sexual encounter becomes easy with minimal planning. Creating this foundation requires attention and effort, but is well worth it in any long-term relationship.

14

Health and Hygiene

Being fit and healthy is an important part of a vibrant sex life. Adequate sleep, a nutritionally balanced diet, and regular exercise all contribute to the way we see ourselves, how we cope with life's stresses and, especially, how we relate to intimate others. A strong body promotes a strong mind. A healthy mind promotes a healthy body. There is plenty of medical research to validate that mind and body can no longer be thought of as operating independently from each other.

After five years of marriage, John had become pleasantly plump. He was winded after going up a flight of stairs. He was lethargic most of the time after work. All he felt like doing was eating dinner, watching TV, and going to sleep.

Corrine was frustrated. John never seemed to desire her sexually any more. By the time the kids were settled, John was snoozing on the sofa. Sometimes he would awaken in the morning with an erection, make a flirtatious remark, and Corrine's hopes would go up. If there was any sex at all, the experience was rushed and unsatisfying as John's mind turned quickly to his day's work. Work was an arena in which John felt comfortable. Deep inside, John felt very uncomfortable with the way he looked and felt. In truth, John felt he wasn't sexually attractive to Corrine, so he wouldn't arrange the sensual dates for Corrine the way he used to when he looked and felt more attractive and virile.

Although John knew regular exercise would be helpful, he couldn't maintain an ongoing exercise program. Corrine suggested he hire a fitness coach. John agreed. He felt much more motivated with the help of his coach. In six months, John lost fifteen pounds and found he had more energy than he had in years. Once again, he liked what he saw in the mirror. John felt a new level of confidence in his sexuality. Corrine was delighted with the new levels of attention she was receiving from John. She was thrilled to get her sexy husband back.

Practice

Purpose: To help you determine if there are any areas you may want to focus on to improve your physical and/or mental health which can enhance your sexuality.

VITALITY CHECK

- **Are you getting the amount and quality of sleep that lets you wake up feeling refreshed and ready for your day?**
- **Is your diet based on complex carbohydrates with adequate protein and no more than 30% of your calories coming from fat?**
- **Do you have some form of exercise at least three times a week that works your cardiovascular as well as your muscular and bone system?**
- **Do you have ways to deal with stress, such as meditation, fog-out time, or alone time?**
- **Do you have a strong support system you can lean on during tough times?**
- **Can you give, ask for, and get both verbal and emotional strokes?**
- **Have you had a complete physical, including blood and cholesterol levels in the last eighteen months?**

If this Vitality Check points to something that needs to be changed, create a plan for that change with daily and weekly steps. Focus on one change at a time. The more healthy and vital we feel, the more energy we'll have for sex. With more vitality, we will not be as likely to hear, "Not tonight, dear. I'm too tired!"

HYGIENE

Practicing good hygiene gives us confidence that we are presenting an attractive package to our partner. We are giving a gift, the gift of self. It makes sense that we take the time to be sure the package is nicely wrapped and inviting.

Bathing for cleanliness is a good start. Some individuals have very strong body odors. Anti-bacterial bath soaps can be used. Be sure to check with your partner for personal preference. Some people prefer the scent of a natural body. Take a shower two or three hours before sexual play for optimal pheromone action. Don't be afraid to ask your partner for what you want in the moment. Coping with the results of being truthful is all a part of the dance of intimacy, getting to know more about each other.

Take a shower two or three hours before sexual play for optimal pheromone action.

Find out about your partner's interest and response to your choice of scents. Deodorants, fragrances, lotions, and hair preparations all have scent. Some individuals may be allergic to these scents.

Good grooming of hair, beard, mouth, teeth, finger and toenails add to the attractiveness of the package you're presenting to your partner. It is not pleasurable to have a sensual moment interrupted when a sharp fingernail or hangnail comes into contact with delicate skin or tissue.

Bathing or showering together can be a joyful and sensual way to begin a love-making session. It gives each person more confidence that they are "squeaky clean."

It is also important to have prepared and "groomed" the area or space in which you plan to play. It feels so good to have clean sheets along with towels or handi-wipes close at hand. Make sure the entire room is comfortable as possible with all the conveniences you desire or may need at your fingertips to avoid breaking the flow of energy and connection between you. We'll go into more detail about ambiance later.

If there are physical limitations, medical conditions, vaginal or urethral infections, it is important to communicate these to your partner so they will not inhibit each other's pleasure or comfort.

If either of you are experiencing ongoing physical/sexual problems, please read Appendix B. You will probably want to consult a qualified professional.

15

Good Sex Is Letting Go

Good sex is about letting go, surrendering to the moment, to your partner and to yourself. People who have a hard time letting go of control, or who are critical of themselves and have low self-esteem, tend to have more sexual problems. For men, this can mean erection or ejaculation problems. Women may find it hard to have orgasms, especially in the presence of their partner.

If we are punishing ourselves or our partner, the quality of our sex will be less. **Sex is about surrender.** If we don't feel emotionally "safe" with our partner, we won't be able to totally let go.

It is important to stay in present time to be fully sexual. Being in present time means taking the maximum amount of pleasure and enjoyment out of what you're experiencing in the moment. This means tuning in and paying close attention to what you and your partner are doing and how you are feeling NOW. A quick, effective way to stay in the NOW and out of your mind is to simply return to your breath. Breathe with your mouth open, and let your breath be your focus and your guide to your senses. If you have armored or turned off your body's sensation, you may need some special help in the form of body-work, or "sensate focus training," i.e., learning to feel with all your senses.

> **A quick, effective way to stay in the NOW and out of your mind is to simply return to your breath.**

Men often feel pressure to "get it up," "to perform." Many men believe sex is intercourse and intercourse can only be successful with a good hard erection, i.e., they can only be successful with a hard erection. When women believe this as well, it can place additional pressure of performance on the man and on the relationship.

Aaron came in for counseling because he was having trouble maintaining his erection. His perception was that his wife, Vicki, had many complaints about his inability to maintain his erection. Although in talking with Vicki, it was clear that it wasn't that big an issue with her. Difficulties began at a time of emotional stress on the family. Aaron was feeling a lot of pressure at work. With each episode of "failure," Aaron became more anxious and more focused on what his penis was doing and not doing. He found that the more he thought about it, the less able he was to relax and enjoy his love sessions with Vicki. After learning some relaxation exercises and some new coping skills that he could use to deal with the pressures of work, Aaron was able to leave much of the stress and anxiety of his day outside the bedroom. He became aware of how much he judged his sexual "performance." Coaching Aaron and Vicki consisted of going back to the basics of "sensate focus" in which they both spent more time on each other's entire bodies. They learned "taking touch" which enabled them to find more pleasure in giving to each other. They discovered that, by focusing more on the pleasure they were giving and taking from each other, they were more able to stay in present time with their love-making. Aaron's attention turned from his penis to how much pleasure he was giving Vicki. Her expression of turn-on and excitement so excited Aaron that erections started to happen regularly.

In addition, Aaron began to more easily receive sexual attention from Vicki, which was very hard for him to do in the past. To his surprise, Aaron found a whole new source of erections and sexual satisfaction by being in a relaxed receiving, feeling, present-time mode. Vicki learned how important her words of support and encouragement were to Aaron. Aaron also felt courageous and confident enough to let Vicki know how much "dirty talk" turned him on. Vicki was happy to oblige Aaron, because she also liked it but was afraid to admit it to Aaron. Both reported "playing, laughing, and being more relaxed and spontaneous with their sexuality."

By focusing more on the pleasure they were giving and taking from each other, they were more able to stay in present time with their love-making.

WOMEN AND SEXUALITY

For centuries, women have learned to turn off their sexuality. Only recently has it been accepted that women are entitled to experience sexual pleasure. For a woman to "let go," to have pleasurable and orgasmic sex, she must feel good about herself and feel emotionally and physically safe with her partner. If there are any withheld angers or resentments, her ability to be relaxed and in present time will be reduced. The "Clearing the Decks" practice discussed in Chapter 11 can be a big help here.

Our society continues to hold a double standard around women's sexuality. If a woman dresses too sexually, she may be considered too provocative or "on the make. "If a woman seems to enjoy sex "too much," or have sex with several men at a time, she is considered "loose" or a "slut." She may feel judged by both men and women. Men who behave similarly, on the other hand, are considered "studs" and may be seen as even more desirable.

Maggie grew up in a mid-western town. Little was ever said about sex, but mom and dad made it clear that "good girls don't." She was caught masturbating at age 6 and had to wash dishes for a month. She also got a strict lecture about little girls who give in to their sexual feelings. As an adolescent, Maggie was very confused. On one hand her feelings of desire were very strong, but on the other hand, her mother's anger and disapproval still echoed in her ears. She would go through periods of time without sex and then explode into enjoyment of sex with many men. She met her husband while she was experiencing one of her no sex cycles. Because he seemed to have a low sex drive, she unconsciously believed he would save her from her voracious sexual feelings. After seven years of marriage, she was still having sex-no sex cycles. All the while, she was becoming more angry and blaming her husband for her dissatisfaction.

Although a very sexual woman, Maggie still felt guilty about her sexuality. Other men were attracted to her and her responsiveness created a conscious contrast between her minimal attraction and desire for her husband and the intense attraction to a few other men.

In individual therapy, Maggie learned to accept and feel good about her sexual self. As she worked through her childhood and adolescent issues, she learned to embrace her sexuality and let go of the guilt and shame. She also came to the realization that she was sexually frustrated and projected her anger onto her husband.

After a few couples' sessions, Maggie's husband refused to attend further sessions. Six months later, they separated. Maggie continued her individual therapy, building self-esteem and confidence in her sexuality. She is currently involved in a relationship which she reports is satisfying her emotionally and sexually.

STRESS, ANGER, AND SEX

For most couples, the decks must be cleared of anger (see Chapter 11) before sexual play can begin. Built-up resentment or anger can effectively block sexual thoughts and impulses. Although some couples love to fight just to make up, most couples find fighting is not a constructive or a consistent way to feel passionate and close.

Prolonged frustration and multiple stressors can also lead to a diminished interest in sex. A hostile boss, money problems, chronic illness in the family, moving, having a child, or a death of someone close can each serve to affect sexuality.

ISD—INHIBITED SEXUAL DRIVE

The rapidly paced life style of many individuals these days has led to an epidemic of Inhibited Sexual Desire (ISD). **Sexual therapists around the country report that ISD is the complaint most often**

118 • *Intimacy*

brought into the office. Chronic feelings and perception of stress focuses the mind in the direction of worry and anxiety. The physiological system tires in the face of "chronic sympathetic nervous system stimulation," i.e., stress. Physiological tiredness is the subjective experience and result.

Although the individual may not lose his (or her) ability to function sexually, he or she may experience little interest in sex and sexual play. Less time is oriented toward sexual thoughts. Less time is devoted to intimate close times with his/her partner. ISD can also interfere with self-confidence and self-concept. The individual may begin to believe that he or she is just not a sexual person or that sex simply is not important.

ISD can lead to performance problems such as erectile difficulties or inorgasmia (not being able to have an orgasm). ISD is treated by looking at the relationship in the context of the individual's life. Is his or her life balanced with pleasure, close friends, recreation, regular exercise, and positive family ties?

Individuals who suffer from ISD may be workaholics, tend to isolate themselves, work long hours, and worry a great deal. They leave little time with which to refuel their emotional tanks with fun and "re-creation." How full are your emotional fuel tanks? **Perhaps you are taking life too seriously—it's time for more fun and play.**

If it seems as though you have no extra time for fun and play, please review Chapter 8, Balancing Our Lives, before going any further.

Practice

Purpose: To practice relaxing while focusing on your partner in present time.
Time: 20 minutes

- **Sit facing your partner (on chairs or on floor).**
  (A good way is to sit close on the floor or on a firm bed: while facing each other, sitting, one partner places his/her legs over the

other. You can have one leg over and one leg under. You will know you're in the right position, if you can hug each other, chest to chest.)

- **Gaze into each other's eyes.**
- **Put your full attention on your partner. (5 minutes)**
- **Communicate warm and loving feelings (with eyes only).**
- **Pick up your partner's breathing pattern. Breathe in unison.**
- **If either of you are uncomfortable or laugh, simply refocus and begin again.**
- **Spend 5-10 minutes talking about feelings, reactions, etc.**

   For example:

   In what ways did you feel comfortable during this exercise? In what ways uncomfortable?

   Were you able to stay in present time with your partner? How did you refocus if you lost concentration?

   Let your partner know, through words, the feelings you were communicating with your eyes.

   With your eyes focused on one another and breathing in unison, did you feel a oneness, a deeper sense of connection? Or was your mind going a million miles an hour?

- **At another time, repeat this process, stopping before talking about feelings, and choose to be sexual, carrying the focused relaxation with you.**

16

Touch to Enhance Your Life

Sexuality and a good sexual relationship are dependent on many things. The primary factor is the overall quality of the relationship. Is there trust in the relationship? Respect? Caring? Clear communication? As we have seen in previous chapters, other qualities such as the ability to give and receive strokes are very important in keeping the love and playfulness alive.

DEMONSTRATING AFFECTION

Another very important component in the quality of a relationship is the ability and willingness to show tenderness and affection. Affectionate gestures may include touching, pats on the shoulder or the buttocks (if your partner agrees that it feels affectionate). It may be communicated with a look, a loving gift, or a card. It might be the tone of voice when you are talking about your partner. Affection is a feeling, but unless demonstrated with a behavior, it will go unheard or unseen, and therefore unknown by your partner.

Mental health professionals have long recognized how critical touching is to overall health, including emotional health. Research has clearly shown that touching can mean the difference between life and death in infants. The authors maintain that touching can also be the difference between the life and death of a relationship.

Affection is a feeling, but unless demonstrated with a behavior, it will go unheard or unseen, and therefore unknown by your partner.

Unlike the Latin, Middle-East and some of the Eastern European cultures, Americans have a large personal physical space outside of which they feel uncomfortable. As with most behaviors, one tends to do what was learned as a child within the context of family and community. Americans tend not to touch anyone outside of the nuclear family. For many families, touch is not available in the family either. For these reasons, individuals vary dramatically in their interest, willingness, and tendency to touch others.

There are also gender differences within our culture. Men and women tend to feel comfortable touching each other if they are in relationship. It is not common or comfortable for most adults to touch those of the same sex. Women may get more of their touch needs met than men because of their more frequent contact with children. Women are more likely than men to touch members of the same sex.

Between two, loving people, touching can be a natural, automatic form of communicating love and affection as well as sexual desire. Because touching is a form of communication, it is important that the touching, the tone of voice, and the body language be congruent. If you appear distracted but are making affectionate touching gestures, your partner may feel confused or discounted.

The largest sex organ on the human body is the skin, approximately 2,500 square inches. Touching can be complete in and of itself. Giving or receiving a loving massage can be a marvelous and total experience. After checking in with your partner's desires, touching can also be a powerful transitional experience into a more sexual space.

The largest sex organ on the human body is the skin.

Walter and Jenny came to counseling. Jenny complained that the only time Walter touched her was when he wanted to be sexual. She came from a family that hugged and touched freely and frequently. Walter's family was much more "formal." Walter seldom saw his parents embracing or demonstrating affection. He explained that neither he nor his younger sister were held much or touched as babies.

Walter, on the other hand, wondered why they were having sex less frequently. He had a feeling that Jenny was trying to avoid him.

Recognizing that each came from a very different, family-touching environment was a big awareness for both. This enabled them to stop making each other wrong and to be able to have more understanding and compassion for the other while they learned a more mutual way of touching.

The Sensual Focus I process (see below) was used to help this couple get in touch with what type of touch and level of pressure felt the best. It was especially hard for Walter to be still and "receive" from Jenny without trying to touch her. Much to his surprise, Jenny helped Walter locate many sensuous pleasure zones on his body. With continued practice, both learned what kinds of touch each most desired, what felt best, and that it was okay to ask specifically for that touch.

Jenny began to relax and to feel more in her body as she learned that Walter delighted in touching her without the goal of having sex. Walter was excited by the new level of openness and responsiveness from Jenny. Their frequency of intercourse actually increased after three months. In addition, Walter was able to receive more physical closeness from Jenny and to feel complete without orgasm.

Practice

Purpose: With practice, and reinforcement, touching can be as frequent *and* as easy as talking.

TOUCHING

- **Sit facing your partner.**
- **Hold hands and establish eye contact (1 or 2 minutes).**
- **Clear your mind, except for the task at hand, i.e., learning more about your personal touching patterns.**
- **Take turns answering each question. Be as honest and complete as you know how to be.**
- **When you are listening, ask questions only to clarify.**
- **Do not be judgmental—just listen and accept.**
- **Acknowledge each other's willingness to risk and talk about these issues.**

1. What are the ways I learned to touch or not touch when I was growing up?
2. In what ways did my mom and dad touch or not touch each other? the other children? me?
3. What do I remember most about their touching behavior?
4. What ways do I like to be touched by you, my partner?
5. What ways do I not like to be touched by you, my partner?
6. Is there any way I currently touch you that you would like me to change?
7. When I touch you, how do you feel about my timing?
8. Do I sometimes touch you too much, or not enough?

9. In what ways can each of us promote and increase loving gestures in our relationships? Be as specific as possible.

LOVEPLAY

Sexual foreplay is the word that is often used to describe the behavior that is a prelude to sexual intercourse. Foreplay is a limiting term. The word implies a second-class status to "real" sex which is the single goal of the foreplay, or "before" play. However, a complete body massage, holding hands, brushing your partner's hair, or giving your partner a footbath can be as loving and lustful as penile/vaginal intercourse. A stimulating intimate verbal exchange can also feel as bonding and as sexual as intercourse. Because we want you to examine all of your feelings, thoughts, and behaviors as having the potential for sexual feelings, we choose to use the word "Loveplay," throughout this playbook. **Let go of your goals.** If there is to be a goal, let it be fun, pleasure and self-nurturing; let it be play.

**If there is to be a goal,
let it be fun, pleasure and self-nurturing; let it be play.**

Melissa and Gary came in for counseling after ten years of marriage. Melissa knew Gary had a hard time touching in a tender way, but her rationalizations to herself had grown thin. She was feeling unloved and frustrated that Gary couldn't hug her even when she asked. As Melissa's anger grew, Gary withdrew even more. After a few counseling sessions, it became clear that not only did Gary grow up in a family where his affection and touching needs were not met, he was overwhelmed by Melissa's level of touching. He couldn't understand why she had to touch him in public. He was also confused about her need to be held and caressed as it related to her need for sexual play.

Slowly, each began to fully accept that men are different than women and that each can be different because of early family customs and teachings. Melissa learned to pace her touching and explain more with words what she was expressing. **Gary was coached** in "taking touch." **He began to touch Melissa because it felt good to him.** He also focused on expressing his reactions with words. He let her know when it was too much.

When in public, Gary learned to say, "Melissa, I know you love me, but I'm feeling embarrassed by the amount of affection you're showing me." "I own the problem and I'm trying to deal with it. Would you please tone it down a bit. I love you, too." He was acknowledging, taking responsibility, not blaming, and asking for what he needed. Gary learned that this is a complete and healthy communication.

Melissa took immediately to the idea of loveplay. She loved all kinds of sexual play. Gary was more conservative in his conceptualization. Penile/vaginal intercourse had always been "sex" to him, while everything else was either foreplay or "to get the woman ready." He was very pleased to find through his work in this playbook that he could work at sex less while enjoying it more and for longer periods. In counseling, Gary began to deeply trust Melissa's love and her desire to share her life with him. The more he allowed himself to trust her love (and his own love-ability), the more he was able to laugh and tease about sexual issues and even laugh in bed. **Sex ceased being a feat to accomplish and much more a process of pleasure.** Touching became a much more reciprocal and frequent mode of communication on multiple levels.

Practice

SENSUAL FOCUS I

The purpose of this practice is to enhance and broaden your giving and receiving skills through touching, a primary means of establishing physical intimacy.

Part A

- **Establish a warm comfortable place to be alone with your partner. Perhaps you would like candles and soft music.**

- Set aside a minimum of an hour or two for both A and B.
- Do this exercise fully clothed.
- After deciding who will go first, sit down facing each other.
- Touch your partner's face tenderly and lovingly. Get to know his/her face intimately.
- Very, very slowly touch her/his hair, neck, chest and arms. How do your fingers feel?
- Please remember to breathe.
- Take approximately 10 minutes. Switch positions of giver and receiver and repeat the practice.
- Take some time to talk about each of your responses, sensations, and feelings in both the roles of giver and receiver.

Part B

To be done on the same day or another day as you may prefer.

- After creating a warm and receptive environment, both of you take off your clothes.
- Sit facing each other (chair or floor).
- Decide who is to go first.
- Giver is to begin by touching her/his partner's face. Then very slowly touch hair, neck, shoulders, breasts, arms, abdomen, upper and lower legs, and feet. (This should take about 15-20 minutes.) Pay attention to details such as skin and hair textures, contours and color. Be sure to give adequate time to each body part.
- Please refrain from genital touching.
- Switch roles and repeat the above practice.
- When this is completed, discuss your feelings, perceptions, and sensations with your partner.

- *Please do not interrupt* your partner when he or she is talking. You are simply listening for understanding to facilitate your ability to be sensitive to your partner's sensual, touching desires.

- Although you may feel aroused, *please, no intercourse.* Discuss with each other alternative ways you can emotionally or physically deal with this arousal without intercourse. Be creative.

17

Self-Pleasuring Is for Grown-Ups

We will be using masturbation and self-pleasuring interchangeably. Masturbation has been accepted as normal behavior during the past five decades by mental health professionals who consider masturbation and genital exploration healthy for young children. It is also normal and healthy behavior for adults. Self-pleasuring broadens the concept to a process of joy and reduces some of the connotations that many of us carry about the word, "masturbation."

Masturbation may be the first sexual behavior about which you learned to feel guilty or shameful. Because few of us receive positive sex messages from our parents, church, or other authority figures, you may have felt confused and torn between sensations that felt very good and the fear that they were very bad.

You may have been punished as a child for touching your genitals. Your guilt and fear may have led to secret times in the bathroom or bedroom trying to get "It" over with before being discovered. These pressures are thought to be an important source of anxiety for "premature ejaculation" problems. Similarly, a young girl's shame and fear may have led to a lack of sexual exploration, subsequently diminished feelings of arousal, and possibly "inorgasmia" (inability to experience orgasm) as an adult.

Because of stereotypic ideas about sexuality, some individuals may consider self-pleasure, i.e., masturbation, to be second-class sex. A spouse may feel hurt or sexually rejected when her/his partner self-pleasures. There may be guilty feelings which can be destructive. However, most couples can learn added ways in which masturbation can enhance their sex life.

For many adults, the word "masturbation" has negative connotations. It may be erroneously viewed as merely a means for a single person to have a sexual outlet or for couples who have a poor sex life. By changing the word "masturbation" to "self-pleasuring," many people have been able to accept masturbation as another positive addition to their sexuality. The authors find it ironic that some individuals refuse to touch their own genitals but expect their partner to want to touch those same body parts.

Self-pleasuring can be an excellent means of increasing body awareness and sensations for both men and women and is a primary tool in assisting preorgasmic women to become orgasmic.

You really are "your own best lover." With exploration and practice, you know just where and how to touch yourself for maximum pleasure. When you are in touch with your body, you can more clearly communicate to your partner what feels good, what pressure and speed to use, and any new areas or techniques you may have discovered to be pleasurably sensitive.

Although many people think of masturbation or self-pleasuring as a genitally-based experience, your entire body is sensitive to various forms of touching and stimulation. Some examples of other areas include breasts, nipples, lips, neck, ears, back of joints, toes. Further exploration may provide some surprises for you, as you wake up your entire body to more pleasure.

For many partners, the sight and sounds of their lover pleasuring her/himself is highly erotic and arousing. Masturbation can be a part of the arousal process, and it does not have to lead directly to orgasm or ejaculation.

You and your partner may have differences in your attitudes, opinions, and feelings about masturbation. It is important to identify and communicate these differences to one other.

Practice

Purpose: To communicate and understand openly your partner's feelings, attitudes, and behaviors regarding masturbation.

SELF-PLEASURING

- **Each partner is to respond and complete each statement before going to the next statement. We recommend you answer questions separately and then discuss all your responses with your partner.**

  Remember: feelings are one-word descriptions of inner experiences. Examples are "apprehensive," "excited," "repulsed," "neutral," "anxious," etc.

1. I feel _____ talking to you about masturbation.

2. <u>Y</u> or <u>N</u>, I masturbate. When I masturbate, I feel _____

   The way I feel about masturbating at this time of my life is
   _____

3. I pleasure myself _____ times a week

4. Some of the issues and experiences from childhood that impact my feelings about masturbation are
   _____

5. What I believe about you and masturbation is _____.

   I feel _____ about your self-pleasuring.

6. Some of the ways we might consider incorporating self-pleasuring behaviors into our sexual life are: (Check those applicable.)

   _____ to arouse myself or you, my partner

   _____ I'd like you to let me watch you masturbate (or vice versa)

   _____ Show me how you'd like to be touched

_____ Playful behavior when partnered lovemaking is in the future (i.e., flirtations)

_____ An invitation to thinking and feeling more erotic

_____ Self-pleasuring when we're apart. Maybe even phone sex.

_____ (add your own) _____

Marie and Doug had been married four years when they decided to seek professional advice. Doug had masturbated almost daily prior to his marriage and found masturbation to be an important source of self-nurturing and pleasure. He felt strongly that his masturbation did not in any way interfere with his sexual desire or love for Marie.

However, Marie complained about his need to masturbate. She believed that happily married men should have no need to masturbate. Marie felt threatened and inadequate when she thought about, or was confronted with, the reality of Doug's desire for self-pleasuring.

Marie and Doug considered their sex life pretty good, but Doug was beginning to feel resentful of Marie's nagging and making him wrong for wanting to self-pleasure. Similarly, Marie was feeling resentful because Doug didn't agree with her and continued to masturbate, which threatened Marie's belief in his love for her.

After establishing rapport, the therapist began to gently challenge Marie's beliefs about marriage and masturbation. Upon questioning, Marie admitted that sometimes she wanted to self-stimulate but had stifled her desires because she believed she should not feel that way.

Some intense sessions about "shoulds," guilt, masturbation, and sex opened the way for Marie and Doug to communicate with less fear and more openness.

When the therapist recommended that each go home and self-pleasure separately, Marie was shocked but agreeable. At the next session, Marie agreed that she had enjoyed herself and still loved Doug, desired Doug, and found pleasure sexually with Doug. She began to believe that maybe Doug could feel that way too.

The next assignment included the two of them masturbating in the presence of the other. After some initial embarrassment, Doug and Marie reported that the experience was very arousing for each and led them into some very hot sexual play.

Practice

Purpose: To support the idea that we are our own best lovers, that we can lovingly give to ourselves as well as our partners.

VISITING ROYALTY FOR SELF

This practice is designed to be done individually. It involves using fantasy to set the stage to pamper and nurture yourself as if you were visiting royalty from a faraway country. Your goal is to roll out the red carpet in order to impress this dignitary in every way possible.

This practice is designed with great care. Please make a point of reading and considering every detail presented. Remember it is for your pleasure.

Setting the Stage

- **Set a time frame of a *minimum of two hours*. This does not include preparation or setup time, which may range from one to two hours. There are two major areas on which to focus your attention. The first is your environment; the second is yourself.**

- **You may choose a special room or your whole house, depending on the amount of time available. A bed or flat surface with pillows to recline on will be needed. Prepare your environment by cleaning, decorating, or using any props that would make you, the royalty, feel celebrated and comfortable. Think ahead to include any items you may need for your experience. Have them within easy reach so your mood won't be interrupted. Pay special attention to music, lighting, candles, pillows, lotions,** oils, a hand mirror, sensuous foods, drinks, and any other props you might like to include for you to feel special. Bouquets of flowers add a very festive touch.

- After the environment is prepared to receive the royalty, it is time to prepare yourself. Pick some loungewear that is sensuous and comfortable. You may wish to create a costume or use ornate scarves. Have everything easily available to you after your bath.

- Take time arranging the bathroom so it reflects the same mood as the other rooms you have prepared to receive royalty. Soft music, champagne, candles and bubble bath all help to set the scene.

Focus on you — Enjoy!

- Now, relax into your bath! Use this time for any shaving, fingernails or toenails. Nurture yourself. Take your time. When you feel complete, start your dressing process using the chosen scents, jewelry, or other special accessories. Please remember to keep it soft, sexy, and sensuous. Men, this is a great time to experiment. Let your imagination play!

- As you complete your dressing, move to the mirror for a look. Use the mirror and your eyes to reflect *only the positive* things you see about yourself. Use these moments to acknowledge the great preparation you have done in readying yourself and your surroundings.

- You are now ready to move to the specially prepared area that includes a bed or flat surface. If you have not already, turn on any music you have chosen and soften the lights or use candles. As you lay down, take a few moments to breathe, to relax, and tune inward. If you find your mind wandering, focus on your breathing and on the music.

- After a few minutes of relaxation, slowly begin to lightly stroke your hair with your fingertips. Take your time. Use differing pressures and notice which feels best. Go slowly. Notice, as well, what you are feeling in your fingertips. You will notice that the lighter you stroke, the more you will feel through your fingertips. If you press too hard, the pressure deadens some of the delicate nerve endings. See what pressure works best for you.

- After several minutes move down to your face with the same slow and sensuous strokes. Focus down to small areas around the eyes, nose, chin, lips, cheeks, and throat. This is your chance to nurture and explore this royalty, to find new and exciting ways to be nurtured that you can pass on to your partner.

- Continue the same slow, sensuous exploration on your chest, arms and stomach. You may have to take off some clothing or attire at this point. Men, your nipples can be just as sensitive as a woman's. Use this time to caress your breasts just as you would your woman's breasts. Spend plenty of time finding just how you like to be touched. Remember to take the feeling in through your fingertips with each stroke.

Further Exploration

- For both men and women: As you come to your genitals, pick up your hand mirror and begin visually exploring your genitals from every angle. Take your time. Raise your legs high enough to be able to see you anus. (A pillow under your lower back may help.) Carefully notice all the detail there. Remember, this is just to explore and become more aware of your genital area. Look with the curious eyes of a child. This is not about judgment or comparison. Breathe through and let go of any anxiety or shoulds you may experience.

- After several minutes, begin slowly stroking your genital area with a very light finger stroke. Pay attention to the sensitivity of each area as you go. Take your time! Use a lubricant if you desire. The slower you go, the more sensuous and nurtured you will feel. You are your own best lover. Nobody knows your body like you do. You are gathering information about yourself that you can pass on to your partner. Allow yourself at least fifteen minutes for this part of the process. Remember, your goal is exploration and sensuous pleasuring, not orgasm.

- Women, be sure to locate your clitoris and pull back the hood to view the head and shaft of the clitoris. Notice where you are most sensitive and how much pressure feels best. Men, do the same with the head of your penis. If you are uncircumcised, pull back the foreskin and slowly explore for areas of sensitivity.

- Women, slowly start to explore your vagina. You may desire some external lubrication for comfort. Visualize your vaginal opening as a clockface. Work around the entire clockface, (12:00-11:00). Notice what "hours" feel best and with what pressure.

- For both sexes, this is an ideal time to explore your anal area. Lightly and slowly caress the anal ring. You may explore your rectum by slowly massaging the anal sphincter with a well-lubricated finger until it relaxes enough for your finger to easily slip in. There is no rush. Notice what feelings and sensations come up for you. Note your comforts and discomforts. Use your breathing to help you relax through any discomforts.

- Continue down your thighs with light brush strokes. If you feel tickled at any point, note it, and then try to go beyond the tickle. You may be in for a very sensuous experience. Pay special attention to the back of the knees, the toes, and the bottoms of your feet. Use your hand-mirror to assist you in viewing areas you may not be able to see directly. Continue to experiment with different pressures and strokes. Remember this is royalty you are pleasuring. Give him/her the best!

By now, you are probably immersed in sensuous, turned-on feelings. If you wish, go back to your genitals and practice peaking, i.e., coming up to the point of orgasm and stopping just before ejaculation or orgasm. After the intensity of the feeling subsides, begin again. Do this at least three times before you give yourself an orgasm. You will experience an intense release! Give yourself plenty of time to relax and take in the total pleasure of your experience. Later you may want to share your experience and feelings with your partner.

You can use this practice any time to nurture and acknowledge yourself and to learn more about your body. By sharing your experience with your partner, your level of receiving pleasure and intimacy will dramatically increase. Enjoy!

18

Advanced Pleasuring When You're Ready

As a couple feels more emotionally and physically bonded, they often want to explore additional areas of sexuality. Two common sexual variations are oral and anal sex. With so many books and information about sexuality being available, the stigma and judgment about anal and oral sex are diminishing. Sexual surveys indicate that more people are incorporating these behaviors into their sex play than ever before.

This chapter can assist you in feeling more comfortable with oral and anal sexual practices. We wish to stimulate thoughtful and intimate conversation and to help open new possibilities for your sexual expression.

ORAL SEX

Oral-genital sexuality can be exceedingly pleasurable. As we will see in a later chapter, kissing and touching all over the body can be sensual and arousing. Every woman and every man is different. Preferences regarding pressure, stroking direction and speed will differ among persons and specific situations. We recently saw a woman who had been married many years and rarely permitted cunnilingus. Once she had permission to tell her husband exactly what felt good and what did not, she began enjoying it to such an extent that it became a frequently enjoyed part of their loveplay.

Individuals, including those in partnership or marriage, may feel differently about oral sex, i.e. cunnilingus and fellatio.[1] As with all sexual behavior, cultural, religious, and gender-related beliefs create taboos, permissions, and specific preferences regarding oral sexual behavior.

Early hygiene training may have inappropriately included the belief that the female genitals are "unclean or dirty." Women, young and old, are given little or no permission to explore their genitals. A mature woman may not know what her genitalia looks like. If she has looked, she may think her genitalia is ugly. The taboos about masturbation may have further prohibited her from exploring the sensations of which she is capable of experiencing. This may lead to arousal and orgasmic problems. If a young woman was forced or pressured to give or receive oral sex, she may feel a lack of desire or even revulsion towards oral sex.

Masturbation is enjoyed frequently by many young men. According to the 1993 Janus Report, 9% of 20 to 30-year-old men masturbated daily, whereas 20 to 30-year-old women masturbate daily at the rate of 3%. Men frequently fantasize about oral sex with women. Many men report that their favorite sexual experience is either cunnilingus or fellatio, i.e., giving and receiving oral sex.

With the pervasive, confusing, and often shameful beliefs, as well as prevalent gender differences in attitudes toward genitals, it is easy to see why men and women may have ambivalent feelings about oral sex.

Although most of us have no taboos about kissing with the lips, the mouth is very rich in germs, i.e., more than the female vagina or male urethra and penis. The male and female urethra is very low in bacterial count, not at all "dirty." A freshly bathed penis or vagina is

---

[1] Cunnilingus is the act of using the tongue on the female genitalia. Fellatio is the act of using the mouth on the male genitalia.

very clean. There is little or no odor associated with healthy vaginal secretions.[2]

Mutual inhibitions often prevent couples from talking about sexual details and specifically about their desires. For example, once a woman has said no to fellatio, the man may never bring it up again. She may be apprehensive about considering a change in her own attitude or behavior, or be concerned that her husband would be displeased or suspicious if she proposed a change. She may change her mind, but she will use her own projections (of fear and disapproval) to keep her from bringing up the topic of oral sex.

Healthy and happy couples talk about what they like or might like sexually. Marriage can last for many years. The best way to avoid boredom in the long run is to have a broad and ever-growing repertoire.

The best way to avoid boredom in the long run is to have a broad and ever-growing repertoire.

THE PROSTATE, THE MALE G SPOT

The prostate is a gland in the male that lies directly below the bladder. It is about the shape and size of a walnut. The prostate continually produces a secretion which make up the greater part of the semen. With patience and practice, many men will experience a very pleasurable feeling when the prostate is gently massaged manually, externally or internally.

The technique for massaging the male G spot internally is similar to the female G spot. Gently insert a *well lubricated* finger (or fingers, for advanced practitioners) very slowly in the anus, palm up. Reach up towards the belly button with the pad of your finger. The prostate

---

[2]Should you or your partner notice an unpleasant odor from the vagina, you may wish to consult a physician because it may be the sign of an infection or other medical condition. The healthy vagina is clean with no discharge and essentially no odor.

will feel like a nodule (about 2 to 3 inches inside the rectum. Remember to go *very slowly* and gently at first, getting continuous feedback from your partner. Helping him to relax his breathing will also help him relax his anal sphincter muscles.

Once the prostate is located, gently rub the prostate using a "come here" motion with your finger(s). Many men can actually have an orgasm with prostate massage. It will feel different than their normal orgasm, but much the same feeling that women describe about their G spot orgasms. An added benefit of prostate massage is that it seems to promote and maintain a healthy prostate. Since a very high percentage of men acquire some form of prostate disease by the age of 70, this seems to be a simple way to promote prostate health.

THE FEMALE "G" SPOT

We now know that different portions of the vagina vary in sensitivity and thus vary in the way each area contributes toward arousal. The female G spot is one of those areas, identified as being more sensitive. G is for Graefenberg, the physician who first identified the area. The G spot is often called the sweet spot. Some sexologists, including Dr. Gary Schubach now believe the G spot is, indeed, an area and can vary greatly in size and sensitivity.

The G spot is approximately an inch in diameter (may be larger or smaller in a specific woman). It is most often found down and behind the pubic bone, roughly opposite the clitoris. Stimulation of this spot for many women heightens arousal and increases the intensity of sensation and orgasm. The G spot can be stimulated with fingers with or without a partner.

Many women can experience G spot stimulation during penile-vaginal intercourse, but many cannot, because of the physiological fit of penis and vagina. Penile penetration (from the rear) of the woman's anus can often stimulate the G spot when conventional intercourse cannot, because of the angle of the penetration during anal intercourse. For many partners, this is an added bonus to the pleasures of anal intercourse.

ANAL SEX

Anal sexual play can be highly stimulating and satisfying to both partners when done with care, communication, and proper information. The area surrounding the anus is second only to the eye in the number of nerve endings, so there is potential for a highly erotic and pleasurable experience.

Some may view anal sexual play as dirty because the rectum is associated with the body's elimination process. In order to feel more comfortable if these feelings are present, we would recommend reading, *Anal Sex and Health,* authored by Jack Morin. Anal bathing or enemas are highly recommended before play to feel comfortable and even more relaxed. It's really not any different than bathing the rest of your body before lovemaking.

Others may have tried anal penetration and found it to be painful. Normally speaking, penetration is painful only if the receiver isn't relaxed or there has been some kind of trauma to the anal area. It is up to the giver to be very sensitive to the receiver by going very slowly and gently. Communication between each other is essential. A key rule is: **There is no such thing as too much lubrication!** With enough lube and sensitivity, the anal sphincter will learn to relax and thoroughly enjoy the loving attention. Use only water-based lubrication inside the anus/rectum.

There are many forms of anal sexual behavior worthy of mention. Analingus (rimming) is using the lips and/or tongue on the area around the anus. With a casual sex partner this would be considered unsafe sex. With your marriage or other committed monogamous partner, this can be highly arousing and safe when hygienic precautions are used. Finger play with your partner's anus can also be enjoyable. Rubbing of the buttocks or other sensual touch of the buttocks can enhance any sexual behavior with either sex.

Penetration of the male by the female, i.e., with finger(s) or toys is the only sexual act available that can promote the feelings of vulnerability that a woman has during "normal" intercourse when a man enters her body. This can be an opportunity for the male partner to empathize more completely with his woman's experience of being penetrated.

> **With anal sex, as with all loveplay, there must be communication, mutual interest, and consent as well as a playful attitude and an open heart.**

With anal sex, as with all loveplay, there must be communication, mutual interest, and consent as well as a playful attitude and an open heart.

With experimentation, patience, relaxation, and a large amount of lubrication, any form of anal sexual play can be very pleasurable. There are many more behaviors that loving couples may mutually choose to include in their loving play. Other sexually oriented behaviors you might wish to consider are briefly described in Appendix C.

Human sexuality is a plethora of thoughts, feelings, and behaviors. It is what you want it to be and probably more. It is the recovering of that "natural child," who experiences without judgment. It is the complete integration of mind, body, and spirit. It is the play of the adult, the wonder and curiosity of the child.

Sexuality is continually renewing itself and evolving as an experience. **To be fully sexual requires only the desire be on the journey,** i.e., the motivation, and then the follow through or effort. **This playbook is a road map.**

Practice

LOVEPLAY:
THOUGHTS AND FEELINGS ABOUT ORAL AND ANAL SEX

> **Purpose:** To encourage increased self-exploration and open, complete communication about feelings and behaviors as they relate to oral and anal sex.

Part A: Oral Sex

1. I feel _____ (anxious, excited, etc.) when I think about talking about oral sex with you.

2. I feel more/less comfortable (or the same) talking about fellatio than I do about cunnilingus. Why this might be so is

   _____

3. The way I learned and/or experienced fellatio was

   _____

4. The way I learned and/or experienced cunnilingus was

   _____

5. My current feelings about fellatio with you are

   _____

   What I like best. What I like least.

6. My current feelings about cunnilingus with you are

   _____

   What I like best, what I like least.

7. In order for me to enjoy cunnilingus more, I need

   _____
   (e.g., gentleness, time, talking, softer, harder, etc.)

8. In order for me to enjoy fellatio more, I need

   _____
   (more pressure, last longer, patience, more lead time, instruction, etc.)

9. Some of my wild and crazy thoughts about oral sex and our love making are _____

   _____ I'd love to orgasm during oral sex.

   _____ I love losing myself in your _____
   (appropriate genitalia)

   _____ Can we try 69, i.e., mutual, concurrent oral sex?

   _____ I like receiving oral sex best when _____

   _____ I like giving oral sex to you best when

   _____

(For those uninitiated) I would consider giving and/or receiving oral sex if _____

Part B: Anal Sex

1. I feel _____ (anxious, silly, cautious) when I think about talking to you about anal sex.

2. I feel more/less comfortable (or the same) talking to you about receiving anal stimulation.

3. I feel more comfortable/less comfortable talking to you about giving anal stimulation.

4. Some of the messages I received as a child about anal sex are:

   _____

5. Some past experiences I've had with anal sex are:

   _____

6. My current feelings about experiencing anal sex with you are:

   _____

7. In order for me to enjoy (or consider) anal sex with you more, I need

   _____

8. Some of my wild and crazy thoughts including anal sex in our love making are:

   _____
   Describe any thoughts, behaviors, turn-ons or fantasies.

9. I feel _____ about talking to you about anal sex.

10. Some questions I've wanted to ask you about anal sex are:

    _____

11. Some areas of curiosity for me about anal sex are:

    _____

12. Some judgments I have about anal sex are:

_____

13. What turns me on about anal sex is:

_____

14. Some fears I want to talk to you about anal sex are:

_____

15. Some health concerns I have around anal sex are:

_____

Gary and Judy had been married six years when they came to counseling. Judy's complaint, initially, was that over the last one and a half years Gary's desire to be with her sexually had diminished to two or three times a month. In the course of their sessions, Judy disclosed that she used to have anal sex with an old college boyfriend. She would get highly aroused which would quickly lead to orgasm. Because she knew Gary had a negative judgment around homosexual men and anal sex, Judy had been afraid to tell him how erotic it was for her.

While doing the "clearing the decks for good sex" practice under the safety of a counseling session, Judy admitted her enthusiasm for anal sex.

Although Gary was startled at first, he opened to the idea of at least talking about the possibilities of some forms of anal sex. Beginning with just rubbing Judy's buttocks with massage oil, these practices proceeded to include fingering her anus, gently inserting his fingers (with lots of lubricant), and later the use of a plastic plug during penile/vaginal intercourse. After a few weeks, Gary agreed that he was aroused by the idea of anal intercourse but was apprehensive that he might hurt Judy. They agreed to proceed slowly and to communicate concerns and specific directions. At the last session, both Judy and Gary were pleased with their expanded knowledge and enjoyment of anal sexual behaviors and felt their overall sense of intimacy had increased markedly.

Regardless of the dynamics with a particular couple, the authors are advocating education, awareness, mutual consent, and openness. All of the topics in this chapter are part of the broad spectrum of sexuality and can be the basis for increased communications about sex. As a result, re-negotiation about what each likes, dislikes, and is willing to try may be necessary as you get new information and develop new attitudes while working your way through this playbook.

When you were a baby and a small child, you experienced more of your natural sexual self than probably at any other time in your life. You were innately curious and had no qualms about tasting, touching, smelling and playing with anything or anyone. These were the years of innocence! As you grew older, you found areas of your own body as well as areas of other's bodies that you were not allowed to touch. Certain areas of your body had to be hidden. Your parents, church, and society let you know what was right for you and what was wrong. You may have begun to feel guilty or ashamed about some actions and some of your thoughts about your body, sex, and someone else's body.

Because of your early programming, it may take some time for you to be comfortable with your sexuality. This playbook can be very helpful. **It is very important to be patient with your partner as well as yourself.** You cannot unlearn all your old beliefs and habits in a few short days and learn new ones to replace these. Go easy on yourself. Give yourself lots of nurturing permission to explore. Create a network of supportive, sex-positive friends who can guide and coach you. There are many books and workshops available on all aspects of sensuality and sexuality. Please refer to the Appendix for more information.

The only goal is personal and relational growth through staying open.

19

Giving Yourself Permission to Be Fully Sexual

James and Jean had been married for four years. Jean called our office complaining that she and James hadn't had sex in over a month. The more she tried to engage James in sex play, the more distant and resentful he became. When they arrived for their first session, James was deeply embedded in his "cave." This made Jean feel emotionally abandoned and angry.

After taking family histories, it was evident that Jean came from a family who was very comfortable with touch and a high degree of emotion. James' parents were very critical of each other and of James and his younger sister. His parents would yell and fight with each other. These behaviors scared James to the point he would run for his room (cave) and lock his door until the ordeal was over.

In addition, James never received any sex information from his parents or in school. He always felt shy around girls. Jean was the first woman with whom he had a long-term relationship. Since sex was something James believed he "should" know about, and Jean believed that all men do know about it, the issue was never intimately discussed. While James was very sensitive to criticism, it was much harder for him to hear the strokes and acknowledgments that Jean used to regularly give him, but had virtually stopped as her anger and frustration level rose. James and Jean used the "clearing the decks for good sex" process and worked hard to learn to give and receive verbal and physical strokes from each other. As part of their homework assignment, they read several books on basic sexuality together with plenty of time for discussion afterward.

James learned that Jean's emotions were a real part of her basic heritage and that he could listen, understand, and validate them, but he didn't have to agree with Jean or "fix" her. Both James and Jean learned "reflective listening." By reflecting back to the speaker what the listener had heard, both felt really listened to and understood. They discovered it gave them a way to correct or amend anything that wasn't perceived accurately. Intimate conversations became more enjoyable.

Jean learned to ask more specifically for what she wanted from James in order to let James know what kind of support or help she needed. James felt emotionally more secure this way, and he really "got" that he didn't have to fix her.

Both found they were more comfortable talking about sex without guilt or fear of judgment. As a result, James felt more confident in pleasing Jean and trying new experiences from both giving and receiving positions. Their sex became more playful and passionate. The frequency level of their sexual encounters increased with a new sense of emotional and physical closeness. By the way, Jean and James' growth took about one year.

Increased awareness of yourself and your body's responses can help you become more comfortable, confident, and skillful sexually. In addition, you will view sex more positively without feeling ashamed or embarrassed when you talk about sex. You will know more about what your partner likes and how s/he feels about sex on deeper levels. To be fully sexual, it is important to be willing to risk trying new thoughts and behaviors. As you and your partner explore new attitudes and actions, it is important to establish a safe supportive atmosphere. This can be assured by listening carefully, letting go of judgments, and keeping yourself open to new ways of thinking and playing. Stay in touch with each other regularly, verbally and non-verbally, practicing good communication skills (see Chapter 3).

As you feel better about all the parts of your body and give more permission to use your body as a pleasure giver and receiver, you will feel more sexually alive. The energy you put out to the world will be that of aliveness, joy, and fullness. Your body deserves to be touched and pleasured as often and in as many ways as is consensual to both you and your partner.

A healthy person sees all sex from a positive perspective, although personal participation in a particular behavior is always a choice.

A healthy person sees all sex from a positive perspective, although personal participation in a particular behavior is always a choice. The sex-positive person sees that the only limits to sexuality are those imposed by experience, knowledge, willingness to fantasize, communicate, and explore. Mutual consent is a mandatory part of any couple's sexual play.

Next to giving yourself permission to be fully sexual, nothing is more important than having a partner who is willing, open, and supportive. If we feel judgment, criticism, condescending humor, or any other form of lack of support, there won't be much of a chance for exploring new or deeper forms of sexuality.

Behaviors which may be uncomfortable for some people include all forms of oral sex, anal sex with or without penetration, sexual behavior with same sex partners, sexual behavior with anyone outside of marriage, sexual aides, birth control, certain positions of intercourse, masturbation of self or another, to mention a few. The list is virtually endless.

You may have some strong preferences and opinions. Remember that you are okay just the way you are. Making these issues explicit with your partner gives you the opportunity to examine your beliefs and desires. You may choose to modify your beliefs as your information base broadens.

David and Jane came to therapy after ten years of marriage. Their sex life had virtually disappeared. Both were under extreme work stress and tended to blame one another for the least little thing. As Jane became more attacking, David withdrew sexually and emotionally. Jane also complained that when they did have sex, it was always the same. She wanted David to be more imaginative. David countered that he had once asked if she would fellate him and she refused. He was reluctant to try again.

In the session, Jane explained that she used to feel repulsed at the idea of fellatio or cunnilingus, but that she was now much more open to trying new behaviors. In the course of counseling, Jane admitted that the idea of putting his penis in her mouth was unpleasant. We discussed the messages she had received from childhood about genitals being dirty. Jane and David were pleasantly surprised to learn that genitals are very clean. As part of their homework, each agreed to complete Sensual Focus II (see below) while adding an element of using one's mouth to explore his/her partner's genitals. Both agreed to stop and talk if one of them asked to stop.

As Jane realized that many women really love to give to their partner through fellatio, she began to reconsider her position.

At the time of the next session, Jane and David agreed they had explored new and pleasurable territory, and both wanted more. **Information *plus* permission *plus* behavior change promotes attitude change, not to mention increased passion.**

Please review the questions—and your answers—in Chapter One about the kinds and qualities of the messages you received from your parents when you were a child. Keep your responses in mind as you read this section.

Practice

SENSUAL FOCUS II

This practice is designed to further facilitate physical intimacy. You may experience new sensations and combinations of feelings. Remember that your skin is the largest sex organ of the body. Get to know and feel it.

- **SET ASIDE A MINIMUM OF ONE AND ONE-HALF HOURS WITH YOUR PARTNER.**

- Remove your clothes and sit facing each other. Say hello with your eyes. Honor your partner and tell him/her that you love her/him.

- Each partner is to take turns touching his/her own face, hair, shoulders, etc. Take about ten minutes.

- After you have completed this exercise with yourself, discuss your feelings and thoughts with each other.

- Using the instructions from Sensual Focus I, Chapter 16, page 114, repeat the total body exploration of your partner. Include the genitals if your partner agrees.

- When it is your turn to receive, be aware of your feelings, thoughts, and sensations. Are you distracted? Are you thinking of other things? If so, gently refocus and receive as fully as you can.

- Should one partner not agree to include genitals, repeat the rest of the exercise and respectfully discuss feelings, concerns, and/or apprehensions.

- After reversing roles and completing the practice, again discuss your feelings and thoughts as both giver and receiver.

- Please refrain from sexual intercourse, at this immediate time. We have asked you to refrain from intercourse in this exercise to increase your ability to focus on the sensuality of the touching experience. Because so many of us are performance- or goal-oriented, it can be a completely new experience when we change the goal. Should you wish to have intercourse the next day or so, please feel free. You have our total and complete permission to be fully sexual.

1. Did your feelings and/or sensations change during the exercise? If so, how?

_____

2. Which was easier—to give or receive? Does this represent a pattern?

3. Communicate with your partner what moments were most comfortable and delicious for you.

_____

_____

4. What were the most uncomfortable moments? In what ways?

_____

_____

5. Communicate moments or experiences that were most pleasurable and/or arousing for you.

_____

_____

20

Thinking Passionately: You Are What You Think

OUR MOST POWERFUL SEX ORGAN, THE BRAIN

Although most people may not consider the brain a sex organ, you would find that, without your brain, you would be unable to link the pleasure of sensation(s) with the experience of being sexual with your partner. Can you imagine enjoying a sexual encounter without the sensations of taste, smell, sight, touch, sound, and fantasy? Pretty dull! Humans are the only mammals who choose when and with whom they will be sexual as well as anticipating, feeling, and thinking about the experience. **Isn't that wonderful?**

Loveplay starts with an idea, clearly a mental process. It becomes very important for both the male and the female to know how to create sexually oriented thoughts and how to keep those the center of attention. Without the generation of pleasant, sexually oriented thoughts, one's interest in sexual play will more than likely decrease over time.

Within your mind lies an unlimited source of creativity to keep your sex life HOT and PASSIONATE throughout life.

Within your mind lies an unlimited source of creativity to keep your sex life HOT and PASSIONATE throughout life. Passion can be defined as an intense range of feeling or emotion for someone or something. We can be passionate about sex, about our partner, or about our work. "Erotic" comes from the Greek, "eros," meaning sexual love. Our erotic thoughts are shaped by experience and the customs of our culture. Both passion and eroticism are important to a strong and healthy sex life. They also have magnetic qualities that will draw your partner to you and keep the juices flowing over the years. Your willingness to explore and play is the only limit.

The picture in your head is what you believe reality to be. If you change the picture, you can change your reality. Similarly, if you want to think more passionately, you can choose to do that. Should you choose not to think sexually directed thoughts, sexually oriented behavior will probably be less frequent or less important in your life than for someone who frequently thinks sexually and sensually, and who desires to share these experiences with their partner.

When two people meet for the first time, the major determining factor for the attraction is the "fantasies," that is, the thoughts generated by one's brain. Often we hear, "he/she fits my picture." This "picture" is created by each of our brains based on previous experience. Part of the excitement of a new relationship is finding out how closely this new person meets the pictures we've created in our minds. Ideally, this process will continue on deeper and deeper levels throughout the life of the relationship.

AMBIANCE

Ambiance is creating the environment in such a way that it produces a certain mood or feeling tone. This is especially important when setting a sacred space for intimacy or lovemaking. This can be as important as good personal grooming. **Create an environment in which love and play can flourish.** Be sure the kids are handled so there won't be any interruptions. Turn off the phone and the television. If you are usually sexual in your bedroom, pay special attention to what the room looks like and the scent that is present. (Refer to Visiting Royalty practices.) Candles, music, incense, and color can set a special mood. PLEASE *never fight in the bedroom*. If you are going to argue, then do it in another room. Save your bedroom for fun and sleep. If your house is big enough and you can create the privacy, you might want two bedrooms, one for sleep and one for adult loveplay.

Waiting until 10 or 11 P.M. at night to be sexual is only inviting problems.

Being tired undermines good sex and your good humor. Waiting until 10 or 11 P.M. at night to be sexual is only inviting problems. Be sure you pick a time that you and your partner are feeling rested and energetic. After all, you want to give your partner the best of you. Spending intimate and sensual time with your partner on a consistent basis is essential for the growth and maintenance of your relationship. (See Chapter 8 for more details.)

When the two of you have set the time to be together for sexual play, ANTICIPATE! Use the time to let your mind consider the juicy and erotic possibilities. Perhaps you can remember a recent sexual encounter that was especially satisfying. Recall some "hot frames" that excited you. Feel it in your body! Isn't it fun to recall that time and those feelings? Enjoy your body's reactions to your imagination. Maybe you and your partner would like to act out a fantasy. (More about fantasy in the next section.)

Because you are each unique, what turns you on will vary. Many factors come into play: societal mores, religion, education, gender, fashion, fads, etc., dictate what's sexy or erotic, not to mention the effect of mood and energy level.

ROLE OF FANTASY

A fantasy is a mental image. "Fantasy" is a generic term for a picture in one's mind, a thought with images, sometimes called imagination. One can have a love fantasy, a playful fantasy, or even a hate fantasy. In one sense, all our thoughts are fantasies, including our concept of reality.

There is nothing wrong or bad about your specific fantasies.

One way to use your mind to enhance sex play is with the creative use of fantasy. It is important to realize that we each fantasize and that there is nothing wrong or bad about your specific fantasies. You don't have to act them out. You don't have to judge either yourself or your partner for any fantasy. Keep in mind that it's just a story from the mind of your partner. It may excite you, scare you, or bring up any number of feelings.

The basis for a strong and fun-filled sexual fantasy life is taking the time to know and trust your partner by communicating deeper and deeper levels of your sexual thoughts and feelings.

Lea and Glen had been married for seven years. Their sexual relationship was pretty good during the first three to four years of marriage, and then, inexplicably, Lea's interest and sexual desire began to wane. Both were feeling frustrated and irritated. As their story unfolded, many elements came to the fore.

Glen had been very sexually active before marriage. He enjoyed his masculinity, masturbated frequently, and had a rich sexual fantasy life. Lea had been shy with men and had only one other sexual partner before meeting Glen. Her love and the physical attraction for Glen fueled her passion initially. Over the years, these factors faded. The passion and the desire for sex had, likewise, faded. Both Lea and Glen acknowledged they loved each other, but the spark was gone.

In counseling, Lea found she had a very vague and sparse sexual fantasy life, although she was very creative with her imagination in other arenas. Looking deeper, she admitted she was not sure sexual fantasies were okay. She had read somewhere that fantasies about men other than her husband was like having an affair. She did not want to do anything immoral or hurtful. After a few detailed discussions, Lea decided to let fantasies be merely "play," with the full knowledge that the only man she wanted to be sexual with was Glen.

Glen helped motivate Lea with encouragement, excitement, and permission. Initially, Lea's fantasies were vague and lacked details. However, she rapidly began expanding her fantasies after reading several books of female erotica. Little by little, she gave herself more permission to "play'" with her mind and share her fantasies with a receptive Glen. She enjoyed the "turn on" and was very pleased with herself when her interest in sex went up. Needless to say, Glen was pleased also. They particularly enjoyed the playfulness of the exercise in this chapter.

You may find that some of your fantasies do not fit with your partner's preferences. Let that be okay. You are a different person and have the right to your own fantasies. Fantasies are only fantasies, i.e., pictures in your mind. They can be enjoyed as imagery without bringing them onto the stage of life or experience. The choice remains with you and your partner.

In order to pleasurably share your sexual fantasies with your partner, you must feel safe from judgment, ridicule, or criticism. By revealing your sexual fantasies, you are opening up a deeply intimate part of yourself. If you feel that you may be judged or rejected, you won't be able to let yourself open to share the rich potential for increased pleasure and passion.

You can check out your partner's interest in exploring sexual fantasies by using the idea of a third party. For instance, "Some people were talking at the office or the club, etc., today about masturbation, hot sex, etc. What do you think about that?" Or you might refer to a group of people who were discussing an aspect of sex. If you are already using fantasy, at any level, you may wish to expand it.

Practice

SEXUAL FANTASY I

    Purpose: Explore together sexual fantasy

- **Set aside a half-hour.**

- **You'll need twenty (20) sheets of paper and two pens.**
- **On four (4) sheets of paper, describe an exotic physical location.**
- **On the second set of four sheets, describe on each sheet any combination of people (a twosome, a threesome, or a more some).**
- **On the third set of four sheets, describe four sexual activities or behaviors.**
- **On the fourth set of four sheets, describe four different sexual feelings, e.g., hot, turned-on, erotic, aroused, desire, etc.).**
- **On each of the last four sheets, describe one prop you would like to include (e.g., candles, vibrators, massage oil, foods, costume, x-rated videos, etc.).**
- **Keep sets in separate stacks. Shuffle each stack so you won't know where your responses are.**

1. Taking turns, draw one sheet from each stack. You will each start with a set of five.
2. Using the descriptions, create and share a sexually oriented story. You can do one or up to five stories each.
3. This is meant to be playful and perhaps silly. Enjoy! Let go of your fears and play!

Take time to discuss with your partner any feelings that came up for you during this practice. What was comfortable? What part was uncomfortable? What might be some possible reasons for the discomfort?

Remember: Romance is surprise and thoughtfulness. Use this practice to add some spice and delight.

21

Arousal and Desire: It's More Than Biology

Desire is: wanting, yearning, lusting, craving, or coveting. It is the hunger or appetite for your partner. Desire can be stimulated by the mind through the use of thought, fantasy, or the senses. Desires can be created by your partner's arousal, your partner's stimulation of you, or by self-pleasuring. In our culture, generally speaking, the male feels more desire and attempts to arouse the female's desire by stimulating her to arousal. As women give themselves permission to think, act, and feel more sexually, their ability to sexually desire their man increases. If a woman is having a problem with desire, it is usually an indication that she is dealing with some sort of emotional or psychological pain. It could be some buried angers or withholdings towards her partner, or day-to-day stress. It might be the pain of some prior sexual wounds. A competent sex therapist could benefit both the woman and the relationship. Of course, this is equally true if the male is having difficulty feeling desire.

Desire is the precursor to any sex or loveplay. It can be driven both by your mind and your body. Your mind might be thinking of a previous sexual encounter. It might be dreaming of the deep, loving connection you feel with your partner. It could be a fantasy you want to have or experience. It could also be your body chemistry (feeling "horny") that is calling for the touch and closeness of that special person in your life. This brings to mind the story of the man who came home feeling desire for his wife oozing out of every cell of his body. When he approached his wife, she explains, "Oh dear, not tonight. I'm too tired." The man without hesitation, replies to his tired wife, "Honey, give me five minutes to entice you. Desire can be kindled from a spark to flowing passion with loving attention and hot desire from one partner."

Chuck and Maria came to counseling after fourteen years of marriage. Both their children from previous marriages had left the nest, one to work in another town and one to go to college in another state. This left Chuck and Maria with more time for each other. They discovered that neither really knew the other anymore. They had forgotten how to play together. There was no lusting, craving, or yearning for each other. Sex had become routine and occurred only three to four times a month.

Maria didn't feel desired by Chuck. She had gained twenty pounds over the years and seldom took the time to look attractive or sexy according to Chuck. Maria responded by saying that she hadn't had time while she was raising her family. Besides, they had grown beyond "that" stage of their relationship. She restated that Chuck seldom took her out to a place she needed to "dress up" for, and besides, his golf with the boys was more important anyway. Communication between the two had become short and businesslike. Intimacy was gone! The desire for sex was gone!

In the first few sessions, it became evident to Chuck and Maria that they had taken the focus away from each other years ago. Chuck focused mainly on work and golf. Maria's focus was on home and family. Maria acknowledged that she felt that the "honeymoon cycle" was over, that dating and sex happened before the kids came along. She felt resentful that she was made responsible for Chuck's son, especially after having to be a single parent for two years before marrying Chuck.

As the years went by, she quietly withdrew from Chuck because it seemed that the only time he wanted to be close was when he wanted sex. Maria didn't feel desired. She felt used! Chuck felt used, too. He felt that if it wasn't for his income and his fix-it abilities around the house, he wouldn't be in Maria's life. Years ago Maria stopped trying to communicate her wants and feelings to Chuck because she didn't feel he listened, and she feared being criticized or put down by him.

The initial focus in counseling was to create an environment of emotional safety in which both could share their feelings and wants while feeling validated and understood. This took weeks. They were given structured homework assignments that had them sharing more feelings and more about their wants and visions in their relationship. This helped them get to know parts of each other that had lain dormant for years.

Maria decided to join a health club and invited Chuck to come with her. They found to their surprise that exercising together four days a week was fun. They termed it "their special kind of sex."

Chuck started to take a new interest in Maria as she started taking better care of herself and feeling more energetic. They set up a date night. One week Chuck took Maria out. The next week Maria took Chuck out. Chuck cut back on his golf and enrolled them both in a ballroom dancing class (something Maria had wanted to do for years).

After four months, during one therapy session, they were encouraged to share their sexual fantasies and desires with each other. At the next session both reported with surprise at how excited each got as the other shared their fantasies.

As Chuck heard some of Maria's fantasies, it "clicked" with him that she was a sexual, desirable woman. Maria reported that Chuck was now making it "safer" for her to explore dormant parts of herself without fear of criticism or "put down." For the first time in her life, Maria said she felt like a "total woman."

After the dance class, Chuck and Maria enrolled in a tantra sexuality workshop. To her surprise, Chuck found a form of spirituality that felt comfortable to him and Maria and which enabled them to explore deeper levels of their spiritual and sexual union.

The previous chapters have looked at some of the complex interactions between two people that we are calling "Loveplay." Loveplay can lead to sexual arousal. Arousal is the total body/mind response that generates the interest in being sexual and moves the lovemaking along. Arousal is a process that is part biological response, part psychological anticipation, and part of the movement of energy between two people.

Both the male and female psyche have important roles in the arousal system. Your beliefs and attitudes, as well as specific thoughts and images, i.e., fantasy, can be arousing or inhibiting. To feel arousal, the mind must think sexual thoughts and create sexual images. Alternatively, arousal can be mostly physical, if you get the judgmental mind out of the way. The term for this is "psychogenic arousal." Foreplay includes all the thoughts, behaviors and expectations experienced before a sexual encounter. It could begin days before a sexual encounter! Feeling, thinking, or acting sexy creates and maintains a readiness for arousal.

To feel arousal, the mind must think sexual thoughts and create sexual images.

For both the male and the female, the hormone—i.e., neurotransmitter, testosterone—is responsible for that "turned on" feeling of desire. Testosterone stimulates the brain's pleasure center to increase those psychological signs of increased focus, pleasure, and well-being. There are differences in the female and male arousal patterns that are noteworthy.

Males tend to experience arousal more easily and more quickly than females. Most men can become more aroused by visual and physical stimulation initially. The male sexual response system appears to be more driven than the female because of the presence of larger amounts of testosterone.

Initially, women are usually more aroused by emotional or psychological stimulation, especially when testosterone levels are low. Testosterone levels in women are highest at the time of ovulation and just before menstruation. This frequently coincides with a higher interest in being sexual for many women. It appears that **for a woman, the more sex she gets, the more she wants; and the less she**

gets, the less she wants. Being sexual stimulates her hormones and her thoughts of sex. Thoughts and feelings get old and cold without the stimulation of hormones or psychological/sexual materials.

As has been discussed throughout this playbook, it's important to be able to create sexually oriented thoughts and images without guilt or fear. It is equally important to be secure in the knowledge that fantasies/mental images can enhance rather than detract from your sexual and love relationship. Without generating pleasant sexually oriented thoughts/images, one's interest in sexual play will likely decrease over time.

Testosterone diminishes with age. The power of the human mind can more than make up for this decrease, with motivation and practice.

The following practices will give you the opportunity to feel, think, and share ways that fantasies can be used to enhance desire and arousal.

Practice

SEXUAL FANTASY II

>   **Purpose:** To experience desire and arousal by exploring a sexual fantasy each of you has enjoyed, and share feelings and responses.

- **Set aside a minimum of thirty minutes of uninterrupted time.**

- **If one or both of you have not had a sexual fantasy in the past, now is the opportunity to give yourself permission to create a sexual fantasy, or refer to the previous chapter. Each partner takes turns responding to the following statements/questions.**

1. Take a few minutes to get in touch with a favorite sexual fantasy. Then share a sexual fantasy with your partner. Let it be as short or long as you desire—the more detail, the more the senses are involved, and the greater the potential turn-on.

2. Remember to be a loving, accepting listener when you're in that role. This includes body language, facial expression, and tone of voice, not just words. Try to get in touch with your partner's enthusiasm, so you can really appreciate her/his pleasure and share in his/her arousal.

3. After each partner has shared his/her fantasy, both discuss your feelings, reactions, and thoughts about this process.

4. What did you learn about your partner? What did his/her body language say?

5. What did you learn about yourself? What was different than your expectations? What was the same?

6. How safe did you feel sharing your fantasy? What would you need from your partner or yourself to feel even safer?

7. Is this a process you would like to have more of in your relationship? If so, how might sexual fantasies be a part of your sexual relationship?

Remember fantasies are just fantasies, generated by our creative mind. The arousal energy that can be generated by a fantasy can be used lovingly and pleasurably within the context of a committed relationship.

Fantasies do not need to be acted out to bring passion into the relationship. Acting out a sexual fantasy, i.e., role playing, is another category of sexual play. Enjoy!

22

Loveplay, Every Day in Every Way

The amount of time spent in loveplay before intercourse can be another source of conflict for couples. Men and women often have inadequate information about what a woman wants and needs to be ready for intercourse. A recent study shows the average amount of time spent in sexual play is 15 minutes and the average amount of time of intercourse is 10 minutes, for a total of 25 minutes.

Ideally **loveplay can start hours before an actual lovemaking session.** It might even start days before, especially if distance separates the couple. This type of "foreplay" can provide an exciting buildup of feelings and anticipation for both parties. It involves first "touching" the mind with words, cards, phone calls, looks, innuendoes, dress, and touch. This can generate romantic feelings, or feelings of desire that support many women to feel "turned on" and make the transition to sex. Remember, women respond and get aroused more by emotional stimulation in foreplay.

After romantic, loving behavior which leads to hugging and kissing, a woman may be ready for genital play. When she begins to lubricate, she is probably not ready for intercourse, but she is definitely ready for more stimulation. Most women are optimally aroused and orgasmic after 35-45 minutes of loveplay. Discuss with your partner your specific preferences. Experiment with different amounts of time before intercourse. It is important for the woman's pleasure that she feel the man is enjoying himself while she is receiving pleasure. If the woman is concerned that the man wants something else, is bored, or just wants intercourse, she will not relax or focus and allow herself to receive; therefore she won't move into an aroused state.

GIVING PLEASURE AS A TURN-ON

Do not forget that a major source of turn-on and arousal for both women and men is turning on and pleasuring one's partner. It is quite common for men to initiate, get "on a roll," and forget how exciting it can be for his partner to give to him. Similarly, a woman may be unaware of how her partner gets turned on by giving to her and experiencing her arousal. Loveplay presents an excellent time for each partner to practice being passive and receiving.

RECEIVING

Receiving can be an uncomfortable role for someone who excessively gives (or controls). Giving to one another can also be an opportunity for the partner who may feel unsure about ways to touch or nurture to gain confidence and skill. The practice of receiving can turn into excitement. Practice! Practice! Practice! The fear of receiving is usually based in childhood shame and feelings of not deserving or being "good enough."

BEING A TAKER

Another way to look at the roles of giving and receiving is to be a "taker" in either role. If you are in the traditional giver role, think of yourself as *taking* pleasure for yourself as you touch your partner's skin and feel a sensation coming through your own fingers, tongue, etc. *Taking* your own sensations as a result of touching your partner will enable you to continue for longer periods of time since there is a feeling of inflow of energy as well as outflow to your partner.

The receiving partner can think of him/herself as "taking" the feelings of pleasure. In this way, receiving becomes a more proactive position. This attitude can help the more passive partner to feel a greater sense of equality and participation. Because we are conditioned by our culture to not have "too much pleasure," there may be fears of being selfish or self-centered if one is the "taker." However, a maximum amount of pleasure can be had by both partners when each is "taking" their pleasure from the other. Give yourselves some time to experiment with this concept. The results will be gratifying!

SLOW AND LIGHT TO MORE DELIGHT

One way to experiment with this new way of thinking is to **use a new, lighter, and slower touch with your partner.** The nerve endings in the fingertips are very delicate. More pressure tends to deaden some of the sensitivity available. This is easily demonstrated by touching the back of your hand ever so lightly and slowly. Notice the sensation on the back of your hand and your fingertips. Next use a harder and faster stroke on the back of your hand. You probably noticed that you felt more pressure, but less sensation. Experiment with various speeds and pressures, but remember, the lighter and slower the touch, the greater the sensation for both "takers."

Practice

Stop and discuss, specifically as possible, the types of stimulation and the amount of time you enjoy loveplay. Women tend to enjoy about 30-45 minutes of loveplay. Men may request and require less. Only you know what you desire and the ways your body responds.

Answer and elaborate with one another:

1. Do I give (or receive) most comfortably?

2. I would like to practice receiving (or giving) more?

3. Sometimes I'm not honest with you about what I really want.

Yes ____ No ____ Give example

_____

_____

4. The amount of time I like to spend in loveplay is

_____

5. The kinds of loveplay I like best include

_____

_____

POSITIONS

There has been much positive change in the perspective of American couples toward positions of intercourse. In general, couples today feel more comfortable experimenting with different physical positions and in unique locales than did previous generations. The female superior (woman on top) position has increased in popularity as women often find it to be more pleasurable for them. This is probably due to her increased ability to move around and locate her "sweet spot." Men often prefer the female superior (on top) position because he may be able to maintain an erection longer. Some men report that it is harder to maintain an erection with the woman on top. You are each very different and can only find your favorite positions by experimenting and communicating with your partner. Be willing to use your imagination, be playful, and experiment. If you want more complete information about sexual positions, many books listed in the Appendix can be useful resources.

ORGASM

For many, orgasm (ejaculation for men) is the only goal of their loveplay. This perspective is limiting. If you are focused on a future event, i.e., your orgasm, you are taking yourself out of a present time experience and robbing yourself of much sexual pleasure in favor of a few moments of orgasm. Men may be trying to delay orgasm and be totally consumed in that endeavor and thus avoid communication and intimacy in the moment. Women may be mentally consumed by the question of whether or not they can orgasm before their partner gets bored. One or both may be trying to reach mutual orgasm. These activities are anxiety producing and rob each partner of pleasure in the moment.

Most of you would agree that bringing the maximum amount of pleasure to your partner and to yourself is what you *really* want. **When pleasure in the moment is the focus, you will find orgasms coming more naturally and easily.**

Both men and women can discover the greater joys of arousal and orgasm by practicing "**Peaking.**" Peaking is bringing your partner or yourself to the point of orgasm and then backing off by stopping, reducing, or changing the stimulation. By going through several cycles of peaking, you can actually improve the intensity of the total experience including the intensity and length of the orgasm.

An orgasm does not have to be the signal to stop loveplay. An orgasm can allow both of you to focus on additional pleasuring in a variety of ways including cuddling, sharing feelings, appreciations, and other "afterglow" activities.

Practice

Purpose: To share with your partner feelings and thoughts about intercourse and orgasm.

Take turns answering the following questions.

1. What I know about myself and orgasm is
   _____

2. My favorite position is _____ and why
   _____.

3. My least favorite position is _____.

4. My favorite place to make love is _____.

5. A position I've always wanted to try is _____.

6. A position I've been afraid to try is _____.

7. Some of my biggest fears about my orgasm are
   _____.

8. My fears about your orgasm are
   _____.

9. I have/have not faked orgasm with you. This is how I feel now about faking orgasm _____.

10. List three (3) behaviors that you could do to enhance pleasure and reduce emphasis on orgasm.

    * _____
    * _____
    * _____

AFTERGLOW

Some individuals find it difficult to resist sleep after orgasm, but can learn to stay awake with a little practice. There is a neurotransmitter released after orgasm which promotes sleep. It appears to be more prevalent in the male, but a woman may also feel sleepy after orgasm.

Afterglow can be one of the most sweet and intimate parts of any lovemaking session. It can be a time of quiet reflection of moments of deep emotional, spiritual, and physical connections.

Many couples find it wonderful to hold each other and reassure each other of their love at this time. Afterglow time is a very special time to simply feel your feelings and share them, with words and touching. There is a special closeness when you have been sexual with your beloved. This is an optimal time to open your hearts to experience fully your sense of loving and being loved.

MINI-PRACTICE

Stop and discuss what behavior(s) you prefer after being sexual. Be honest with each other. Now work out a mutually agreed upon set of behaviors for after sexual play. Maybe you would like to cuddle or hug or fall asleep in one another's arms.

23

Keeping It Playful for Eternal Loving

Partners in successful, satisfying, long-term, intimate relationships describe behaviors and feelings which connote or are symbolic of the closeness they feel. They may have pet names for each other. They may have playful, loving rituals they engage in regularly. There may be special communications that represent discussions, exchanges, or experiences over time but have the power to bring the partners together when conflict or a major difference threatens their deep connection.

For example, Joe and Mary learned over time that they could chide each other gently using very formal versions of their names which served to remind each that he or she was behaving in a rigid, controlling, i.e., parental way. When Joe calls Mary, "Mary Elizabeth," she knows she has gone beyond his boundary of appropriateness. This is her cue to back down, usually with a smile and an apology.

Couples who have been together for a long time often describe a special kind of humor and play that characterizes their relationship. It is part of their "coupleness." Each would miss this element intensely should the partnership terminate. We believe that loving, playing, and sexuality are intimately interrelated. **Playfulness enhances all of life. It keeps us feeling and acting younger.** Playfulness reflects and supports a sense of freedom and exploration, all of which are critically important in a happy, fulfilling and sexually satisfying relationship.

Couples who play may not be aware of it. It may be difficult to identify what they do. It is a shared perspective on the world that includes inside jokes and feelings of really knowing and being comfortable with another. Intimate play is characterized most by the attitude of playfulness mixed with laughter. Give yourself lots of permission to laugh at yourself and your partner. It's laughter done with genuine affection. It says, "aren't we silly, or isn't it fun to be human?" It is really another facet of intimacy when two people share this level of play. Do you smile when you think of your partner? If you do, you probably have some form of intimate play in your relationship.

It is very difficult, if not impossible, to teach someone how to play. Although we can offer descriptions, it is very challenging to consider teaching playful behavior because of the personal nature of it. It may be difficult to develop and enhance intimate play. It may be challenging to even see it. Playfulness comes from the little child within. Remember a time, as a child, you had a really good time. What was special and fun about that time? Upon consideration, you may find components of innocence, curiosity, playfulness, and silliness without judgment. Identification of the obstacles to being more playful can be a beginning to adding more intimate play into your relationship. Then it is important to identify the doorways to play.

Is not romance a form of intimate play? Discuss with one another and identify the ways the two of you already engage in intimate play. If there are none, give at least two examples you have seen with your friends that you would consider intimate play. Hint: What are they doing when they laugh together? Consider Gloria Steinham's dictum—"do something outrageous (silly or fun) every day."

GETTING FROM "TURN OFF" TO "TURN ON"

"Turning on" is what this playbook is about—turning on to self, partner, life, and sex. Personal and relationship growth is a process that takes time. By getting in touch with your inner child, it is easier to think and act playfully. Every flower you stop to smell and admire, every cloud that fills you with awe, every joke you allow to tickle your funnybone, every daydream in which you indulge, plants the seeds for "turn on."

Each of us brings into our relationship values, attitudes, and beliefs emanating from our family of origin as well as the broader society. These beliefs include those about sex and sexuality, relationships, and play. You and your partner do have differences in this arena. With clear, honest, and non-defensive communication, these differences can be examined and serve to enrich our lives rather than be a source of conflict. Honesty with your self and your partner is a critical element.

Practice

Purpose: To share with one another feelings and thoughts about intercourse and orgasm.

- **Set aside 45 minutes.**
- **Be sure you each have a pen.**
- **Take turns answering each question *or* write out all your answers first and then relate them to your partner.**

A. The elements that make intercourse desirable and exciting for me are:

1. Lots of touching ❏
2. A romantic dinner ❏
3. Feeling I am really desired ❏
4. Mutual passion ❏
5. My favorite fantasy ❏
6. No performance demands ❏

7. A new or different setting ❏

8. Candles and music ❏

   The kind of music that turns me on is

   _____

   _____

   _____

   (Fill in your own)

   9. _____ ❏
   10. _____ ❏
   11. _____ ❏
   12. _____ ❏

B. Explain, in as much detail as you can, each item you checked. Alternate if that feels comfortable. Or let one partner describe his/her desires completely before going to the second partner.

C. Discuss an element you would like to include the next time you loveplay. Discuss ways you would like to do that. And DO IT!

CREATIVITY AND PLAYFULNESS

Human beings can be extremely creative. Tapping into that natural, playful, sexual inner child can enrich your sexuality. Remember how you felt on your first date, with your first kiss, or the first time your date touched your genitals. Just using your imagination and memories, you can engage a very sexual, sensual part of you.

Adventurous sex may include props, massage, footbaths, and/or costumes. Creating novel settings, outdoors or indoors, can also be the source of additional excitement. One couple decided to have a subjective kissing contest. Both agreed she won. It was so much fun, they had a subjective oral sex contest. Both agreed he won that one! When they had their sensual massage contest, neither could agree who won, so they declared it a tie and celebrated the rest of the night.

EXPRESSING PASSION

The way you think and feel is critical to being a passionate person. However, if you want your partner to know how passionate you are or wish to mutually share your passion, then it is imperative to demonstrate or show your passion. We're talking about the myriad of behaviors that can be seen as passionate. (See Chapters 7 and 20.)

SEXUAL ENHANCERS

A sexual enhancer can broadly be defined as anything you choose to bring into your environment to augment or improve your sensual or sexual experience.

Dressing in a sexy outfit, such as garter belt and stockings, may be enough for you. Some couples enjoy **playing roles** with each other.

Fantasy can allow you the framework to let go psychologically and enjoy your body and your partner. Fantasy can serve to increase the sense of playfulness in your relationship. Perhaps taking on a new persona for the evening, acting "as if" you are turned on, or newly wed, or have just met, etc., can increase your arousal and focus you sexually. Only you can decide what you want in your relationship. Jan and Dave pretended to be strangers meeting in a bar. They had fun and laughed at themselves for a long time.

Any activity or behavior which can establish the mood of intimacy, romance, and sexuality will be worth exploring. Board games that promote discussion and sensual play can be fun as well as learning experiences. There are many available currently which are directed toward the couple and increasing intimacy such as "Getting to Know You Better" and "An Enchanted Evening." These kinds of games can be purchased at large game stores, adult bookstores, or on-line bookstores.

Dancing can be very sensual and sexual for many individuals. Your body is moving and you are in close proximity to your partner.

Music with a sensual beat may assist you in creating a deeply passionate experience after a couple of hours of "cutting the rug."

SEX TOYS AS ENHANCERS

Vibrators can be a powerful adjunct to any couple's sexual repertoire. Both men and women can use them for arousal. As men get older, they often experience greater difficulty getting a firm erection and maintaining it. A vibrator can often be an important means to maintaining a firm erection for these men.

A vibrator can often bring a woman to orgasm that cannot climax with intercourse or manually. The vibrator can more directly and intensely stimulate the clitoris and clitoral shaft. Vibrators are enhancers.[1] Have fun! Be curious! Find out what works for you.

Dildoes with or without vibrators can be significant enhancers. Regardless of the ways you choose to use a dildo, be sure your partner agrees. One couple enjoys using dildoes to play out their mutual fantasy of group sex with no risk to their monogamous relationship. It is very playful and arousing for them.

Sex toys, aids, or sexually explicit materials may be threatening to a relationship unless there has been open, honest communication and the limits of both parties are discussed and respected. We recommend enhancers only in that they become a positive addition to your sex play, hence sex enhancers. **Remember, this is adult play.**

In the course of therapy with Steve and Shelli, the subject of sex toys came up. Steve became quiet and withdrawn. When this was addressed with Steve, he recalled that early in their relationship Shelli disclosed she was faking orgasms when she was sexual with Steve. She confessed the only way she could have an orgasm was while self-pleasuring using a large dildo-shaped vibrator. Steve was devastated. It took many months for him to trust Shelli again. He felt sexually inadequate.

Shelli reacted by throwing away her vibrator that had brought her so much pleasure. She never brought up the subject of vibrators

---

[1] Some women may find that over-use of strong vibrators may diminish sensation. Simply be aware. Anything can be over-done.

or toys again so she wouldn't hurt Steve. Steve did love Shelli, and, as time went on, his pride healed, and they both worked together so that Shelli started to have orgasms through oral or manual stimulation. Deep underneath, Shelli missed the stimulation, visual excitement, and variety that her old friend, the vibrating dildo gave her.

In therapy, Shelli was able to tell Steve her long-standing withhold. Steve was able to hear her now, with more confidence. In addition to listening to her, Steve admitted he was getting turned on at the thought of introducing sex toys in their loveplay. With help from their therapist, Steve and Shelli were able to fantasize going to a sex shop together and looking over the assortment of sexual toys just as they might window-shop in any other type of store. By the next session, both were delighted with how they fantasized throughout the week, and they were ready to actually go to a sex store. Shelli assured Steve that he was her best lover and could never be replaced by any toy. They also said they had some of the hottest sex they had in years, as the excitement of their fantasy grew more real.

They decided to each purchase a sex toy of their choice for the other and have a very special date the next weekend to introduce these new additions to their sex play. They acknowledged that both were afraid to broach the subject of toys because of the incomplete transaction of years before. They also made an agreement that if either felt unsafe to communicate about any part of sexuality, they would make an appointment with each other. They would let the other know at the start of the conversation that they were feeling afraid to communicate their feelings as a forewarning to the other partner to be sensitive to what he or she was about to discuss.

Practice

SEXUAL ENHANCERS

Purpose: To openly communicate with one another fears, apprehensions, and doubts about using sexual enhancers. To create greater awareness of your partner's preferences and desires.

Keeping It Playful for Eternal Loving • 179

Remember: This chapter is on playfulness. Keep this practice playful too. Respond to each of the following statements by initialing your feeling position on the continuum. Work separately. There are separate forms for each of you.

    e.g., hard _____ JT _____ OF _____ easy

A.

1. Talking about sex toys such as dildoes, vibrators, etc., is:

    hard _____ easy

2. I'm unsure _____ sure
    of your feelings about sex play and sex toys.

3. I'm afraid _____ not afraid
    of your responses and reactions to a discussion of my desires and wishes about sexual enhancers.

4. a. I don't like _____ like very much
       the idea/use of vibrators for myself.
   b. I don't like _____ like very much
       the idea/use of vibrators for you.

5. What I think about vibrators is _____

    _____

    _____

6. I don't like _____ like very much
    the idea and/or use of dildoes for me and/or for you (circle one or both).

7. Ways I would like to use a dildo are

    _____

    _____

    _____

    (can be more than one way)

8. I don't like _____ like very much explicit videos, magazines, or photos.

   Specifically I like: _____

   _____

   _____

   _____

   When I like to use videos the most is _____

   _____

   _____

   When I like to use magazines or sexually explicit photos is

   _____

   _____

   _____

B. After you each have answered the questions, it's time to sit down with one another. Take plenty of time and discuss each subject in as much detail as you can.

Part of building excitement and anticipation for your sex play can be shopping together or individually for sex enhancers in the form of toys, games, music, clothing, scents, movies, and music. One of the great advantages of sex enhancers is the many new options and opportunities that open up to those who use them. Enhancers can ignite a very routine sex life. You may find yourselves getting turned on just discussing some new toys or other enhancers with which you might want to experiment. The range of possibilities are limited only by your imagination. Have fun!

24

Spirituality and Sex

"Spiritual" is derived from the concept of spirit, that presence in each human that is a copy of and reflection of the life force of the universe, i.e., God, Goddess.

Spirituality is an essential part of the human, as real as the mind and the body. **The spirit is that part of each of us that transcends the mundane and touches the outer reaches of our existence.** It is not religion. Religion is human-created and thus fraught with all the weakness of our species, such as sexism, powerism, guruism, racism, etc. Spirituality speaks to that which is beyond human and is not subject to one man or woman's perspective or opinion.

With maturity, attitudes, needs, and perspectives on life change. One's sense of belonging and connectedness to the universe becomes more of an issue. Mental health professionals, lay authors, and media representatives are openly addressing spiritual matters. This is more likely a result of the general aging of the population and most particularly, to the Baby Boomers reaching fifty. More people are thinking about their own place in the "big picture." When spirit flies free, the core of the universe can be felt. There are many paths to the divine. Religion is but one path. There is much interest, at present, in the holistic, earth-based spiritual practices such as the Native American traditions or that of Celtic origin, with the Goddess representing the great Mother, Earth.

Many Westerners, tired of the repression and shaming of sexuality by Judeo-Christian beliefs, are turning to the spiritual traditions of the East, which embrace the concept of sexuality as the essence of the sacred, and human coupling as touching the divine. Hindu and Tibetan Tantra practices use ritual, prayer, breath, and positions to promote and enhance the expression of sexuality, with the intent of connecting the Chakras (power points aligned with the spinal cord) for the blossoming of the higher self. Taoist sexual practices have similar intentions.

Sex, self, and the higher power are intimately connected.

These approaches share the attitude that sex, self, and the higher power are intimately connected. By honoring the self and the other through sexual union, a most high form of spiritual experience can be manifested. In the ancient Inca tradition of the Andes, Yinanté, i.e., the couple or coupling, is the highest form of being-in-the-world.

Regardless of your spiritual beliefs, it is not difficult to see the ways in which sex and sexuality are part and parcel of our lives, our humanness, and the evolution of all life on this planet. Perhaps it is time we honored all that we are and that, most certainly, includes our spiritual and sexual selves.

It's been said the fastest way to God is through relationship. Allowing oneself to be deeply vulnerable to another brings us back to our original innocence and the power of our divine, pure, spirit self, which demands the exposure and healing of childhood wounds.

When a couple chooses to undertake this journey, they can reach a point where their souls, i.e., spirit selves unite. Spirit or that which is natural (nature-all) is not man made. Sex can be the catalyst for uniting the physical, spiritual, and emotional. It is God creating Itself through a couple. Sex is nature's way of preserving itself. Sex is a very natural and normal part of all that is nature. Sexuality is but one channel to explore spirituality. It involves deep work that many choose not to do. However, when two people on a spiritual path connect, even deeper spiritual exploration is possible through the sacrament of sexual union.

It is interesting to observe that the thrust of modern marital counseling is to use sex and sexuality as both a barometer of the couple's intimacy as well as the focus of the therapy. By focusing on the sexual feelings, thoughts, and behaviors, the couple is pushed to deal with the core issues of the self and the relationship, including emotional intimacy, trust, responsibility, and vulnerability—all essential issues of the spiritual self as well.

PERSONAL GROWTH AND SPIRITUALITY

Personal growth is more of an attitude than a particular thing that happens. As you move through your life, there are ages and stages to contend with. Change and the ability to adapt is the common element throughout. The ways you face the change in your life says a great deal about your attitude(s) and flexibility toward life. Why are you here? What is the meaning of life? What is a "good" life? These are critical questions to ponder, not that there are specific answers or "right" answers to these questions. **It's really more an issue of the process of asking,** and then struggling with the answers, **that ultimately differentiates the conscious human from the unconscious one.**

Growing into a more self-aware person and one who is more aware of his or her impact on the planet and with others is an essential element of personal growth. All the skills inventoried in this playbook are personal growth steps that can lead to the deeper integration of sexuality, spirituality, and the self.

Great personal growth can result from a spirit-filled sexuality. When two people unite sexually, their spiritual energies and physical bodies combine, permitting deep exploration of each other. People grow as conscious selves as they feel safer to surrender, not just to their partner but to the universal force some call God, Goddess, the Creator, etc. This phenomenon occurs as each partner loses him/herself in their experience by intense focus on the partner and within themselves. An example of this surrender and connection is the point of orgasm, when conscious thought is suspended and one is thrown into the cosmos via extreme ecstasy. Some have described this experience as transcendent of body. The greater the consciousness, self-confidence, and love, the greater the potential for profound ecstasy.

To go this deeply with a partner, **there must be deep trust of both self and other.** There must be a letting go or surrender to the feelings, sensations, and the moment. With each step, a couple is pushed beyond their comfort zone, and each is forced to deal with her/his fear of the unknown. Each time we courageously face a fear and work through it, we become more conscious and grow as human beings. Being fully present in the moment creates not only ecstatic sex but spiritual transcendence.

Being fully present in the moment creates not only ecstatic sex but spiritual transcendence.

The following practice is a modified version of a Tantra ritual. If you enjoy it, you may wish to read more about Tantra or attend a workshop in Tantra. (See Appendix).

Practice

CREATING A SACRED SPACE

Purpose: To honor the Self and other. Bringing in the energies you desire and releasing those energies you wish to dispel. To create an atmosphere of love and respect in preparation for loveplay. This ritual can also stand alone, without sexual love play. Allow 10-15 minutes (or as long as you wish).

1. Sit cross-legged facing each other and look into one another's eyes.
2. With palms together, breathe out together, touching foreheads, maintaining eye contact.

3. Inhale as you move your heads closer together maintaining eye contact.
4. Close your eyes. Now lean back to normal position, open your eyes and look deeply into your beloved's eyes.
5. In turn, say a few words to honor the other, e.g., "the sacred/divine within me honors the sacred divine (God/Goddess) within you." "Our love is beauty and unites us, one to another, and to that power greater than us."
6. Exhale again, together.
7. Share a few moments of inner reflection.
8. Each put your left hand on the other's heart and your right hand over your beloved's left hand.
9. Honor your heart/love connection with gazes and words of endearment.

Place candles of your choosing around the room. Incense can be wonderful. With bells and/or drums walk around the bed—verbally releasing feelings, attitudes, and energies.

I (we) release (examples)
- fear
- inhibitions
- rigidity
- aggression
- hostility
- shame
- guilt
- etc.

Then walk around your bed (or space) and invite the spirits, i.e., feelings, you desire to join you. "Come in . . ." "We invite . . ."
- joy
- playfulness
- tenderness
- good listening
- love

consideration
passion
eros
etc.

End this section with a long, close hug.
Okay, you're on your own.
After lovemaking, you might wish to discuss feelings, thoughts, sensations, etc. related to this process.

25

Putting It Altogether for Sexual Ecstasy for a Lifetime

Throughout this manual, we have looked at sexuality to enable you and your partner to discover more about each other and learn ways to re-ignite or expand the depth of your joy and passion. By this point, you have read and played your way through each chapter dealing with many aspects of your sexuality. Our hope is that you are more in touch with your own thoughts, feelings, and desires about sexuality and more sensitive to your partner as well.

At this time, it is appropriate that you review, alone and together, the major points that you want to remember in order to continue creating a playful and adventurous sexual relationship

WHAT IS A HEALTHY SEXUAL PERSON?

A healthy sexual being is one for whom sexual thoughts, feelings, and behavior are a part of whom he or she is. She accepts her sexuality comfortably as she does other parts of her humanness. He is aware of the value of relationship and intimacy as it enhances sexuality. It is a beautiful circle of giving, receiving, experiencing, and loving. Respect for self and other is part of being healthy. Taking care of your physical and mental health is a part of everyday life. All sexual thoughts and feelings are fully accepted and validated (not necessarily agreed with).

The human need for novelty is very great. As you explore your sexuality at a deeper and deeper level, you will find new sensations, awareness, and outcomes every time you share a sexual experience. **When you are a healthy and fully sexual being, your sexual thoughts about sex come and go freely.** You appreciate the attractiveness of others and allow those feelings of arousal to enrich your own sexual thoughts and feelings, and take the "juice" back to your partner. Your fantasies are part of who you are. Enjoy them and share them with your partner for mutual delight, with his/her agreement of course.

As a healthy sexual person, you are able to say "Yes" or "No" without feeling guilt or shame. You understand that all sexual play must be consensual, and the scope of sexuality is as vast as all our imaginations. Sex is playful and childlike. Sex has many moods, from very quiet and subtle to wild and noisy.

You are able to see yourself as a sexual being and take the time to incorporate sexuality into your daily activities. You are able to easily talk about sex to your children and other adults. Finally, you have a healthy respect and reverence for sex and support others around you to view sex in healthy ways.

THE 13 ESSENTIAL KEYS TO SEXUAL ECSTASY

We have picked these 13 KEYS TO SEXUAL ECSTASY as a way to review and summarize the most important topics and chapters of this playbook. Each topic or chapter is like a piece in a jigsaw puzzle. Together the pieces form a beautiful and complete picture. Here, the completed picture represents a couple in a deeply committed, loving, playful, spiritual, intimate, and romantic relationship. Each piece is essential to the beauty of the complete picture.

When appropriate, there will be a notation of a specific chapter that further explains a particular key.

1. Open, Clear Communication (See Chapter 3)

Communication goes on between two people regardless of the words spoken. Body language is usually more significant than words.

Listening is the most important way to tell your partner of your love and respect.

Listening is the most important way to tell your partner of your love and respect. Listen for feelings so you may assist in facilitating his/her process. Listen for understanding. Remember that you cannot listen and think about what you are going to say at the same time. Always stay in the present for most effective communication.

Because men and women process information differently, keep in mind that the conclusions you draw about your partner's motivation and intent may not be accurate. Men tend to be action-oriented and visual in terms of what they remember best. Because many women are more kinesthetic and tend to be more process, i.e., communication-oriented, the woman may misinterpret his actions. The man, in contrast, may not believe the woman when she talks, or he may try to hurry her to get to the bottom line.

The "how" of any communication is always more important that the "what." In other words, it is more important to focus on how the two of you solve your problems, talk to one another, and make decisions than to focus on the specific decision being made. For instance, if your biggest issue is a difference of opinion about keeping track of checks in the checkbook, the money issue is less important than the tone of voice you use with each other, the attitude(s) you demonstrate to one another, and your intent of finding a win-win solution.

2. Intimacy (See Chapter 5)

Intimacy is the experience of feeling secure enough within yourself to share the deeper self, your true feelings of the moment with your partner (or another) in a non-blaming, but totally owning way, in the moment. The immediate consequences can be painful or pleasurable. In a healthy intimate couple, it's usually pleasurable. However, even the painful moments will provide an opportunity for a greater sense of closeness, love, and trust as the two of you courageously struggle with the truth. These are the opportunities that provide the greatest satisfaction of bonding and growth for every couple.

Intimacy is sharing your real self, including your "dark or shadow side" with your lover (or a friend). Only then can you learn that you are both loved and lovable. Keeping secrets will only harbor and keep intact your fears that *all* of you is not okay. The truth is, everything you are is beautiful and lovable. You are a child of the universe.

Trust makes this possible. It is another of the circles of relationship. **Risking with your partner leads to trust,** and trust leads to more risking.

3. Strokes—Support (See Chapter 6)

Compliments and acknowledgments are two important ways individuals can be verbally stroked, i.e., appreciated. Learning to give and receive compliments can be challenging, but worthwhile, for an increased sense of closeness and connection.

Support is knowing your partner is present for you. It's paying attention and using good communication skills with sensitivity as well as empathy. Your partner is human and needs you at times.

Physical stroking, i.e., touching (Chapter 16) is also an important way to let your partner know you care, you're thinking of him/her, and that you enjoy being physically "in touch."

If you were fortunate enough to have been raised in a loving and touching family, you are probably a touching person. Because so many of us are not touching people, you quite likely have married someone who is less touching that you. How lucky for both of you! You each have a golden opportunity to be both teacher and student as you experience giving and receiving.

Many of us were taught early in our lives not to be self-centered or selfish. Many were taught not to accept compliments and to be suspicious of those who freely give out compliments. As a result you may have difficulty accepting compliments or loving behaviors. Rest assured, you are not alone. Learning to receive compliments is a beginning step in learning to receive love, affection, and abundance. Learning to receive physically through sexual behavior is a key step in your progress.

If you have not done the exercise to give and receive to yourself, please do that. (See Visiting Royalty, Chapter 17.) **There is a *healthy selfishness*:** a balance between taking care of yourself and considering your loving partner's needs and desires. When your needs are being met and you are feeling fulfilled, it will be much easier to feel and act in loving and giving ways.

4. Giving Your Relationship and Sexuality Top Priority
(Chapter 8)

It's crucial for everyone to plan time away from the stresses and rigors of daily routines to re-energize and re-create. Vacations, mini-vacations, and specially designated nights or weekends all qualify. We'll briefly describe how each can be used.

A vacation is defined as a minimum of one week in which the main focus is on each other (no kids!). Plan plenty of alone time and a minimum of outside activities. Too many activities can leave you exhausted and feeling less than sexual for each other.

Mini-vacations are periods of two to four days. Travel and preparation time is much less than a vacation, but it isn't spent at home. Ideas include bed and breakfast inns, hotels in the city, or camping in the countryside.

Some couples have been able to designate one night during the week as "their night." This may be spent at home, but the phone goes off the hook and the kids are not around. This gives a couple three to four hours during the week to just "be" with each other. You may use this time in whatever way you choose. It may be to plan a hot sexual romp or just to fog out together with a video, etc. Your choices are plentiful!

Other couples have broadened this concept to include one weekend a month. The focus remains on each other and can be spent at home but doesn't include the kids, any business, or housework.

Give yourself permission to experiment with all these forms of getaways and see which works best for you as a couple. If time and money make more than one vacation a year prohibitive, use the other forms. Getting away together does not have to be expensive.

5. Honoring the Self

In order to build a strong, deep and energetic relationship, each partner must first love, honor, and respect him/her self. Honoring the self means taking enough time to get in touch with spirit, to recreate, to self-pleasure, and to go to new depths of personal truth, growth, acceptance, and understanding. This includes a willingness to access and communicate a specific truth, belief, want, need, or desire. Each partner must see his or her truth as a precious gift that will build ongoing trust, intimacy, and love.

6. Addressing Anger, Resentments, and Withholds in a Timely Way

Keep withholds and resentments at a minimum by communicating them to your partner as soon as possible. Make even the slightest irritation important enough to communicate to your partner. Remember, more often than not, small irritations, when held inside, are the ones that result in unexpected explosions or "dumps" of feelings.

Learn to communicate your anger without attack or blame. If there is a lot of charge, use a third person to discharge your feelings using the "Clearing the Decks" in Chapter 11. If the conversation escalates, use the "Time Out Process" in Chapter 11. Be willing to get through your anger in love. By releasing the anger in a clean and safe way, you are paving the way for satisfying and playful sex.

7. Staying in Love

Recall all the special experiences you did when you were courting each other that resulted in your falling in love. This may have included long lingering lunches, dates to romantic places, long evenings in front of the fire with champagne, special cards and gifts of love and affection, or a special phone call just to say, "I love you." Do you remember how to flirt? Part of romance includes the element of surprise. Have you ever "kidnapped" your partner for a surprise getaway at a secluded, romantic rendezvous?

Variety keeps a relationship young and fresh. The possibilities are unlimited here. Any way that your standard routines are altered will result in variety. This may be in dress, behavior, timing, sexual enhancers, or location. You can expand in endless ways.

Thoughtfulness and acknowledgment of your partner is appreciated no matter how long you've been in relationship. Remember, strokes are the lubrication of relationship. Plenty of strokes reduce the friction of a relationship and ensure adequate deposits to the "Bank Book of Love" (Chapter 2).

8. Maintaining Your Physical Body (Your Temple)

Develop and maintain healthy attitudes and behaviors towards diet, exercise, positive mental states, smoking, alcohol, and drugs. Eat wholesome foods, get adequate sleep, exercise, and meditate. All these practices will help you feel fit and look fit, which in turn will encourage you to feel more sexual. This keeps a positive cycle going. As mentioned earlier in the book, people who have sex more often have a strong immune system and enjoy better physical and emotional health.

Keep stress and anxiety at moderate levels. Build and maintain a network of friends that you can depend on when you need emotional help or support. A strong emotional network is like an emotional bank account. It's always there in case you need it. Hopefully, you won't have to use it too often, but it provides a strong sense of security.

9. Permission and Acceptance

Acceptance of differences is important to the growth and emotional trust developed between two people. Acceptance is not approval, nor understanding. It is simply, "you're okay just the way you are." Needless to say, accepting one's self is important for developing maturity and confidence. **Let go of a "problem" orientation** and move toward a perspective of "abundance."

When acceptance of self and other is complete, there is permission to be the fully sexual, playful, lustful beings you are. With profound confidence in yourself and your love, you can be free to let go and just "be." **Remind yourself frequently how loving and wonderful you are.** Similarly remind yourself of your lover's specialness. With openness and permission, the two of you can co-create a special kind of freedom to explore the never-ending joys of life and love.

Male-female differences can be enormous, but they are also a big part of the "juice" of the relationship. It is important to have a great deal in common, but just enough differences to make it interesting. Mother Nature knew what she was doing!

There are common male and female differences about issues of initiating sex, talking about sex, foreplay or loveplay, and play after intercourse. It is never safe to assume that your partner means what you think she/he means, nor is it safe to assume that you can read his/her mind. Always check it out by asking and clarifying.

10. Risking and Courage

It takes awareness and courage to share your feelings about your partner with him/her when you are feeling them. Talking to each other about feelings is an ongoing learning process. **There are no greater gifts to your love partner than the gift of listening and accepting.**

When communication is open, honest, caring, respectful, and intimate, both the woman and the man will get all the love they want and all the sex they can handle. It is a circle of desire, communication, love and sex. The risks of communicating openly are feelings of anxiety, fear of rejection, abandonment, or the experience of your partner's anger.

It takes courage to have a truly great relationship and an ongoing "hot" love affair. **If you're not scared, sometimes, you're not growing** and pushing for intimacy. There is risking as you try new ways to be with each other sexually. Acknowledge your fears to yourself and your partner, as you challenge yourself to experiment and grow.

Great sex in the context of great love is "heaven on earth." It takes self-examination and a willingness to be vulnerable. Ask for what you want and both of you will reap the rewards. If you don't ask, you may not get that which you want.

11. Play-Full-Ness

Spontaneity and creativity are the essence of our inner child. You're fortunate if you grew up in a home full of laughter. If you grew up in a family where life was a very serious matter, you may have to push a little more for authentic play.

Go to comedy clubs, watch funny movies, read comics every morning. Do something you have never done at least once a month—sexual or not. Remember the funniest thing you ever did—and laugh at yourself all over again. Grab your partner and go away for the weekend without plans. Be less structured with your free time. Be nice to yourself and play in the mud sometimes.

The zest for life is an attitude. "Go for it"—now that's a playful life. Let go of your expectations of sex and give you and your partner the permission to experience yourselves: "Regardless of where this goes or what we do, we'll have fun and it will feel good." No goals, just play—as a child does.

12. Spirituality

Humans are complex, mind-body-spirit, beings. Regardless of your spiritual or religious beliefs, honoring your higher self as a reflection or extension of universal truth, beauty, and power can positively affect your experience of life and your sexuality.

As we saw in Chapter 24, certain traditions emphasize the movement of energy and seek to use sexual energy to support a form of communication with the divine heart.

Honor self, honor spirit, honor all the parts of your lover. When two lovers meet in physical union, it is truly a case of the whole being greater than the sum of the parts.

13. Honoring and Celebrating the Relationship

This is a process that occurs when each partner brings his or her fully participating self to this third entity called "relationship." It's the culmination of each partner's life experiences interwoven with all the skills and topics covered in this playbook. It's an appreciation, acceptance, and sense of gratitude for each other's process in the evolution of the relationship.

It's taking pride in "the team." It's continuing to set new goals and visions for the partnership. It's moving synergistically to co-create in ways that touch and heal others outside the relationship and ultimately the planet. It's knowing when to "take a break," to step back, re-evaluate, to rest and heal the relationship and each other.

Celebrating means taking the time and attention to honor one another by acknowledging special dates and events. It can also be taking the time each week to verbally review with one another the reasons you are glad you are in this relationship.

13[1] Keys to Sexual Ecstacy

1. Open Clear Communication
2. Intimacy: Physical and Emotional
3. Strokes and Support
4. Giving Your Relationship and Sexuality Top Priority
5. Honoring the Self (Mind, Body, Spirit)
6. Timely Addressing of Withholds, Resentments, and Angers
7. "Staying in love" with Romance, Courting, and Passion
8. Staying Healthy and Fit
9. Permission and Acceptance. Male and female differences
10. Risking and Courage
11. Play-full-ness
12. Spirituality: Honoring Spirit
13. Honoring and Celebrating the Relationship

---

[1] We did not try to make 13; it just turned out that way. We are very pleased—13 is a very sacred, very powerful number in many ancient traditions.

Practice

VISITING ROYALTY FOR COUPLES

Read this practice together completely, first.

As a culmination of and reward for the effort you have put forth as you circumnavigated this playbook, we offer you this final practice.

In Chapter 17, you used this exercise to treat yourself as "Visiting Royalty." In this practice, you will be able to focus your attention on your partner as if she or he were the visiting royalty.

Please allow a *minimum of two hours* for the experience, plus the preparation time for your room or home, including bathroom, music, lighting, and sensuous clothing for both of you. Since this is a long practice, it may be wise to have only one partner receive on a given day, saving the other for the next day or soon thereafter. (Please agree on this time before you begin.) This will prolong the pleasure of the experience for both.

- **After the environmental preparation (see Practice, Chapter 17 for ideas), begin with the bath. The idea is to totally serve and nurture your partner. All the bathing, shampooing (yes, women, you might try shaving your partner's face) is the responsibility of the server. Please make it a slow and sensual experience with soothing words as well as promises for upcoming pleasures.**

- **When the bath is complete, softly dry your partner and begin dressing him or her in the sensuous clothes that have been previously laid out. Make the dressing as playful and sensuous as you can. After dressing, you may ask your partner to relax for a few minutes if you have any last minute preparations to make on the room(s) you are choosing for the remainder of the visit.**

- **Bring your partner into the room and sit down cross-legged and facing each other. Take at least three minutes to hold hands and hold eye contact with each other. You may, also, try to synchronize your breathing. From this position, slowly start to stroke** your partner's hair and face with very slow and light strokes. Take yourself on a journey of exploration, concentrating on each square inch of skin. Take in the feeling through your fingertips and experiment with various pressures, but go very slowly!

- Continue to lightly stroke the face, neck, shoulders, arms and chest. Remember, this person you're touching is royalty. Treat her/him with dignity and respect. Since this is the first time this dignitary has visited you, his/her body is new to you, so take your time in exploring. It's okay to ask if there is any spot on which they would like special attention, or a particular stroke.

- As you approach your partner's genitals, take time to visually inspect the entire area with the eyes of a curious child. Women, feel free to take the penis in hand or move the scrotum or move the legs for a better view. Men, don't be afraid to move the vaginal lips or gently pull back the clitoral hood to view the clitoris. Continue your visual exploration down to the anal area, giving yourself permission to slowly take in this part of your "Visiting Royalty" without judgment or shame. You may wish to verbally admire your royalty.

- After you have completed your visual exploration, begin to lightly and slowly caress your Visiting Royalty's genitals with a fingertip stroke. Be sure to cover the whole genital area and do not fixate on one spot at this time. Notice how your partner is reacting to your touch and what areas are more sensitive than others. After you have fully caressed the genital area, you may go over the same area with some warm oil or lotion (vegetable based oils are preferred to petroleum based oils). You may use a slightly heavier pressure with the oil, but check with your Royalty for what feels best. Receiver: be sure to communicate to him/her what feels good and what you would like him/her to do differently.

- Men, after asking permission, you may insert a well-lubricated finger into your Visiting Royalty's vagina. *Caution*: proceed very slowly and sensuously, watching for signs of pleasure or discomfort. Visualize the vaginal opening as a clock face, and use your finger like a clock-hand to check each hour for greater sensitivity and pleasure. Request feedback from your royal queen.

- When you have completed the clock face, slowly pull your finger out and put your attention on the clitoris. Start very lightly and slowly, asking for continuous feedback. Try light strokes on both sides of the clitoral shaft, as well as the top of the shaft and directly on the head. Remember this is about sensual exploration! Do not attempt to give your Royal Visitor an orgasm at this point. Women, breathe in all the pleasure your host is giving you.

- Women, as you are caressing your Visiting Royalty's penis, note which areas are more sensitive on the head, around the shaft under the head, the shaft, and the base of the shaft. Experiment with various strokes up and down the shaft. You may try two hands, some squeezes, or various pressures with fingernails. Again, the purpose is not orgasm, so if your Royalty is getting too excited, stop and let him come down a bit. Slowly proceed to the scrotum. This can be a very sensitive area for some men, so ask for feedback on what pressure feels best and where.

- A light fingernail caress on the scrotum may be very exciting for some men, while others like to feel the grasp of the thumb and forefinger around the base of their scrotum with a gentle tug down on their testicles.

- For both sexes, the next area of focus is the perineum. This is the area between the vagina and anus or the scrotum and the anus. This can be a highly erotic area for both sexes. Usually a light stroke provides the most sensations. Take your time to find what pressure and stroke feels best to your Royalty.

- Continue your stroking down the perineum to the anal area and the buttocks. Try different pressures and strokes around the buttocks (fingernails can be exciting on the buttocks!). Now, bring your focus back to the anal opening. If you wish, after asking permission, using a well-lubricated finger (be sure you have no fingernail extended beyond the end of your finger), using a finger cot or rubber glove, massage gently around the anal opening until you feel the anal sphincter relax enough to permit your finger to enter. Go very slowly and ask for ongoing feedback from your Royalty. At this point, receiver, continue to breathe to relax and gently push out with your anal muscles. This will have the opposite effect of contracting, i.e., relaxing the anal sphincter (See Chapter 18).

- Women, when you find your longest finger *fully* inserted and your partner is relaxed and ready, try to locate the prostate, the male G spot. Yes, it's quite deep. By raising your finger up towards the stomach/pubis, you should feel a walnut sized nodule. The prostate becomes more palpable with stimulation. This stimulation can be experienced as erotic, intense, or even uncomfortable to a man for the first time, so be sure to go slowly and lightly. Try a gentle "come here" motion with your finger. This is usually highly stimulating for many men and can produce full body orgasm.

- Men, do the same kind of anal exploration with your Royalty. By using the same motion with a fully inserted finger, you can reach her G spot and stimulate her the same way as if you were in her vagina.

- Be sure that you do not go back to the genitals after anal play unless you have thoroughly washed your hands with soap and warm water. Some rectal bacteria are not friendly to the vagina or urethra.

- Continue down the thighs with light strokes. Monitor your Royalty's face and body for feedback and continue to ask for verbal feedback as well. It is very reassuring for the host to know that the pleasure he/she is giving is being received fully. Slowly progress down to your Royalty's knees, under the knees, calves, feet, and toes. Be sure to find out what pressure feels best when you get to the bottom of the feet. A good foot massage with lots of lotion is a very sensuous and nurturing experience. Take your time and give your very best to this very special person!

- After you have gone over the entire body of your Visiting Royalty, you may return to the genitals. At this point, your Royalty will be filled with pleasure and turned on. Begin focusing on your partner's clitoris or penis, using the peaking process explained in the Visiting Royalty for self-practice in Chapter 17. At the last peak, take your Royalty over the edge to orgasm if so desired. After orgasm, quietly lay together while taking in all the pleasure that you have shared with each other. Later, share your feelings with each other. Be as specific and honest as possible. You may talk about how you might do this practice differently next time. For instance, you may wish to incorporate some toys or play with different themes. Remember, your imagination is unlimited!

After playing your way through this playbook, you are feeling much freer to talk about sex with your partner as well as think and act more sexually. You are setting aside specific times for sexual contact, because you have learned the well-being and bonding that come from complete intimacy. You have experienced how these feelings of well-being extend outward to create more energy, increased creativity, and more motivation in your life.

Please remember, life is a marathon, not a sprint. Go slowly and sensuously. Become one with your partner, not just during intercourse, but with each and every touch. Let the rhythm and pace build naturally. "Whatever happens is truly okay."

Because of an increase in knowledge and awareness, you can move far beyond the thoughts and feelings that previously were based in negative beliefs about you and your partner's sexuality.

SEXUAL IMPASSE

There may come a time in your relationship that you and your partner reach a point of disagreement or impasse with regards to a particular issue around sexuality. You can't agree on a solution or course of action that feels comfortable to both of you. One of you is feeling a loss or disappointment by not getting what you want. There are several alternative solutions that you may try to overcome impasses.

Begin with talking with each other about the images or pictures that come up for you when you think of the area in question. These may come from an earlier experience or a projective fantasy of what might happen. It is also important to share you fears when you feel them. One approach is to talk to each other about what pictures or fears come up when you think of the area in question. There may be new information available that would enable you to feel better about the particular issue. This may be the time to consult a therapist who can help you look at solutions more objectively. A well thought-out plan that feels comfortable to both parties can be the result.

A second strategy might be to brainstorm and talk about other activities that might prove to be even more exciting than the area in question. This lets you both know that you each want to please each other and are willing to search for pleasurable alternatives. Again, we want to stress the importance of honest communication and a desire to work out solutions that will feel good to both of you. With loving and respectful intent and enough time, you can resolve any conflict or impasse.

Suzanne had been taught as a child that touching her genitals (or someone else's) was very bad. She was reluctant to consider oral sex initially. With increased support and additional information, she and Craig began to very slowly try fellatio. Suzanne was very curious and found that, by feeling Craig's growing erection with her mouth, this encouraged her to explore further.

After addressing her personal issues about self-image and feelings that her body was not okay, Suzanne gained greater appreciation for her body and was more open to experimenting with oral sex. Although she is feeling better about her sexuality and sharing it with Craig more fully, she still struggles with deep ambivalence. She is giving herself more and more permission to explore her sexuality.

Practice the 13 KEYS each day. *Use this playbook over and over again* to remind you of your path. We all slip. We each need reminders. We each evolve at our own pace. Love, accept, and nurture yourself and your partner. Your relationship is the foundation for everything else you may wish to co-create. **The path of a loving, intimate, sexual relationship has no end, no destination.**

Please enjoy each step of your journey with our blessings.

Appendix

Reading List

Anand, Margo. (1989). *The Art of Sexual Ecstasy.* New York: G.P. Putnam's Sons.

Anand, Margo. (1995). *The Art of Sexual Magic.* New York: G.P. Putnam's Sons.

Bach, George, Ph.D. & Wyden, Peter. (1968). *The Intimate Enemy.* New York: Avon Books.

Bakos, Susan Crain. (1992). *Sexual Pleasures.* St. Martins Press.

Barbach, Lonnie, Ph.D. (1984). *For Each Other.* New York: Penguin Books.

Barbach, Lonnie, Ph.D. (1998). *Turn Ons: Pleasing Yourself While You Please Your Lover.* Plume.

Barbach, Lonnie, Ph.D. & Levine, Linda, ACSW. (2000). *Shared Intimacies.*

Beaver, Dan, MFCC. (1992). *More Than Just Sex: A Committed Couples Guide to Keeping Relationship Lively, Intimate and Gratifying.* Lower Lake, CA: Aslan Publishing.

Brauer, Donna & Allan. (1983). *Extended Sexual Orgasm.* New York: Warner Books, Inc.

Brothers, Joyce, Ph.D. (1991). *What Every Woman Should Know About Men.* New York: Ballantine Books.

Buscaglia, Leo. (1990) *Loving Each Other: The Challenge of Human Relationships.*

Campbell, Susan. (1980). *The Couple's Journey.* Impact Publishers.

Castleman, Michael. (1989). *Sexual Solutions: For Men and the Women Who Love Them.* Touchstone Books.

Cauthery, Philip & Stanway, Andrew. (1987). *The Complete Guide to Sexual Fulfillment.* Prometheus Books.

Comfort, Alex. (1991). *The New Joy of Sex.* New York: Mitchell Beazley Publishers.

Cookerly, Richard. (1992). *Recovering Love: From CoDependency to CoRecovery.* New York: McGraw-Hill.

Corn, Laura. (1995). *101 Nights of Grrreat Sex.* Park Ave. Publishers.

De Angelis, Barbara. (1987). *How to Make Love All the Time.* New York: Dell Publishing.

Dodson, Betty. (1996). *Sex for One: The Joy of Self Loving.* New York: Crown Publishing.

Duma, Felice, Ph.D. with Philip Goldberg. (1998). *Passion Play.* Riverhead Books.

Elgin, Suzette Hyden, Ph.D. (1993). *Genderspeak.* John Wiley and Sons.

Farrell, Warren, Ph.D. (1990). *Why Men Are the Way They Are.* New York: Berkley Publishing Group

Farrell, Warren, Ph.D. (1994). *The Myth of Male Power.* New York: Berkley Publishing Group.

Farrell, Warren, Ph.D. (1999). *Women Can't Hear What Men Don't Say: Destroying Myths, Creating Love.* New York: Tarcher/Putnam.

Fromm, Erich, Ph.D. (1989). *The Art of Loving.* New York: Harper Collins Publishers.

Godek, Gregory. (2000). *1001 Ways to Be Romantic.* Naperville, IL: Casablanca Press, Div. of Sourcebooks, Inc.

Goldberg, Herb. (1991). *What Men Really Want.* New York: New American Library.

Goldberg, Herb, Ph.D. (2000). *The Hazards of Being Male: Surviving the Myth of Masculine Privilege.* Wellness Institute.

Goodwin, Aurelia Jones, Ed.D. & Agronin, Marc E., M.D. (1997). *A Woman's Guide to Overcoming Sexual Fear and Pain.* New Harbinger Publishing.

Gray, John, Ph.D. (1992). *Men Are from Mars, Women Are from Venus.* New York: Harper Collins Publishers.

Gray, John, Ph.D. (1994). *What Your Mother Didn't Tell You and Your Father Didn't Know.* New York: Harper Collins Publishers.

Gray, John, Ph.D. (1997). *Mars and Venus in the Bedroom: A Guide to Lasting Romance and Passion.* New York: Harper Collins Publishers.

Haeberle, Erwin, J. (!983). *The Sex Atlas.* Continuum.

Henderson, Julie. (1999). *The Lover Within.* Berrytown, Ltd.

Hendricks, Gay & Hendricks, Kathlyn. (1992). *Conscious Loving: The Journey to Co-Commitment.* Bantam Books.

Hendrix, Harville. (1988). *Getting the Love You Want*. New York: Harper & Row Publishers.

Hendrix, Harville & Hunt, Helen. (1994) *The Couples Companion: For Getting the Love You Want*. New York: Pocket Books.

James, Larry. (1999). *Red Hot Love Notes for Lovers*. Career Assurance A.

Jeffers, Susan, Ph.D. (1990). *Opening Our Hearts to Men*. Fawcett Books.

Kantor, David, Ph.D. (1999). *My Lover, Myself*. Riverhead Books.

Kirschenbaum, Mira. (1998). *Our Love Is Too Good to Feel So Bad: The Ten Prescriptions to Heal Your Relationship*. New York: Avon Books.

Ladas, Whipple & Perry. (1983). *The G Spot*. Dell Publishing.

Lederer, WIlliam & Jackson, M.D., Don. D. *The Mirages of Marriage*.

Leonardi, Tom. (1998). *Secrets of Sensual Lovemaking*. Signet.

Lerner, Harriet Goldher, Ph.D. (1991). *Dance of Intimacy*. New York: Harper Collins Publishers.

Lerner, Harriet Goldher, Ph.D. (1997). *Dance of Anger: A Woman's Guide to Changing the Patterns of Intimate Relationship*. New York: Harper Collins Publishers.

Levine, Linda, ACSW & Barbach, Lonnie, Ph.D. (1983). *The Intimate Male*. New York: Anchor Press/Doubleday.

Lloyd, Joan Elizabeth. (1991). *Nice Couples Do*. New York: Warner Books, Inc.

Love, Brenda. (1992). *Encyclopedia of Unusual Sex Practices*. Barricade Books.

Love, Pat & Robinson, Jo. (1999). *Hot Monogamy*. Plume.

McCarthy, Barry & Emily. (1999). *Couple's Sexual Awareness*. Carroll & Graf.

Moore, Thomas. *Soulmates*.

Moore, Thomas. *The Soul of Sex*.

Muir, Charles & Caroline. (1990). *Tantra: The Art of Conscious Loving*. Mercury House.

O'Connor, Dagmar, M.D. (1986). *How to Make Love to the Same Person for the Rest of Your Life and Still Love It*. New York: Bantam Books.

Page, Susan. *How One of You Can Bring the Two of You Together*.

Paul, Jordan & Margaret. (1983). *Do I Have to Give Up Me to Be Loved by You*. Minneapolis, MN: CompCare Publications.

Paul, Jordan & Margaret. (1989). *Do I Have to Give Up Me: The Workbook*. Minneapolis, MN: ComCare Publications.

Pearsall, Paul, Ph.D. (1988). *Super Marital Sex.* Ivy Books.

Peck, M. Scott, M.D. (1998). *The Road Less Traveled.* Simon & Schuster.

Richardson, Diana. *Love Keys.*

Sachs, Judith. (1994). *The Healing Power of Sex.* Englewood, NJ: Prentice-Hall.

Sanderson, Gregg. (1980). *What Ever Happened to "Happily Ever After?"* Adventures in Living.

Sheehy, Gail. (1995). *New Passages: Mapping Your Life Across Time.* New York: Ballantine Books.

Sherven, Ph.D., Judith & Sniechowski, Ph.D., James. *The New Intimacy.*

Smotherman, Ron. (1985). *The Man Woman Book.* Context Publications.

Tessina, Tina & Smith, Riley. (1980). *How to Be a Couple and Still Be Free.* New Castle Publishing.

Winks, Cathy * Semans, Anne. (1997). *The New Good Vibrations Guide to Sex.* Cleis Publishers.

Wolf, Sharyn, C.S.W. (1998). *How to Stay Lovers for Life.* Penguin USA.

Zilbergeld, Bernie, Ph.D. (1993). *The New Male Sexuality.* New York: Bantam Books.

Sexual Dysfunction

This Appendix is meant to be informational only. It is not intended that any one person or couple see this short section as a comprehensive description nor as a means to solving a sexual dysfunction or problem. Should you and your partner be experiencing any of the sexual difficulties described in this Appendix, it is recommended that you seek the professional assistance of an experienced sex therapist.

Problems of sexual function for men and women often have their beginnings in a lack of information or mis-information. Other important sources of dysfunction are physiological disturbances caused by age, disease or drugs, inhibiting cultural and religious belief systems, and emotional disturbances.

There has been an increased amount of information available about sex and sexuality in recent years. Couples with difficulties due to ignorance or mis-information may find that books or articles about sex, such as described in the bibliography of this playbook, are useful in dealing with any difficulty they may be having.

Sexual functioning is a complex interaction of many factors such as those mentioned in the first paragraph. It is often impossible for those directly involved with the dysfunction to accurately diagnose and treat their own problem.

Males and females generally present different types of sexual complaints or disorders. Men generally tend to experience problems with performance whereas women complain most often about a lack of sexual satisfaction or desire.

DESIRE PROBLEMS

The dysfunction that is on the most rapid increase in our fast paced world is that of desire. What professionals refer to as Inhibited

Sexual Desire may include low sexual desire or aversion to sex. Low sexual desire is often related to a high-stress lifestyle and relationship problems that are not acknowledged. Physiological disorders must be ruled out before psychotherapy and/or couples work can be effective.

Women tend to describe low sexual desire more frequently than men, although this ratio may be changing. Low sexual desire, or being turned off to sex, is often based in inappropriate expectations, beliefs, and inadequate sex, i.e., foreplay. This playbook has addressed many of these issues.

AROUSAL DIFFICULTIES

These disorders are typically ones of performance and are seen most frequently in men. An arousal problem may be called "inhibited sexual excitement." Erectile dysfunction is characterized by partial or complete failure to attain or maintain erection throughout the sexual act. Similarly, it is characterized in women by partial or complete failure to attain or maintain lubrication and swelling of the vagina and labia through sexual activity.

An arousal difficulty which happens occasionally is not a dysfunction. It is most likely due to a life crisis, fatigue, distraction, or illness. It is only when the individual has difficulty with arousal on a regular basis that one should consult a professional.

It is important to distinguish between psychological and physiological causes of arousal problems.

Many medical conditions can be the underlying cause of arousal and orgasm difficulties. Similarly, drugs, illegal or prescribed, or over the counter, can also be a causative agent in arousal and erectile dysfunctions. Recent studies have indicated that in the male over forty years of age, a physiological (or medical) problem may be the chief cause of erectile disorders in 50% of those reporting.

Common drugs which have been known to play a part in erectile and or orgasm difficulties are anti-depressants (Tri-cyclics and SSRIs such as Prozac), blood pressure medications, and medications with sedative effects. Alcohol, marijuana, cocaine, amphetamines, and amphetamine-related drugs can inhibit sexual arousal and erection/lubrication.

ORGASM

Typically men present problems with retarded (delayed) ejaculation or premature ejaculation. Retarded ejaculation is the inability of the man to achieve orgasm/ejaculation during sexual intercourse, or a delay of orgasm after an adequate phase of sexual play. This too can be psychological or physiological in origin.

It is important to remember that with any of the male dysfunctions, the psychological factors rapidly assume a prominent role in the difficulty, regardless of the cause of the initial episode of dysfunction.

Premature ejaculation is a timing problem. It usually refers to a situation in which the male would like to continue having intercourse without ejaculation. Ejaculating "too fast" is a highly subjective judgment. Some factors include temperament, pressure from partner, pressure from self, insecurity, and anxiety. The important goal is mutual satisfaction, not the length of time intercourse takes.

All men experience, at one time or another, some dysfunction. In other words, at some time, a male will have difficulty getting and keeping an erection or having an orgasm because he is too tired, or stressed, or maybe has had too much to drink. If a man experiences his difficulty with an erection as a failure or a threat to his masculinity, it is likely that his psyche will promptly compound the difficulty with negative judgments. As almost any man has discovered with time, the more a man tries to get an erection, i.e. brings his conscious mind into the process, the less likely it is that he will get one.

Women present various forms of inorgasmia, i.e. the inability to achieve orgasm. It is quite common (it's estimated about 30-35%) for women to not be able to experience orgasm during the act of intercourse. This is not generally considered a dysfunction unless the woman is concerned by it. These women are usually orgasmic with other types of stimulation.

Inability to have an orgasm at all appears to be often related to a lack of information or misinformation leading to erroneous beliefs. Women are taught to be passive and relinquish control, supporting the idea that the man is in charge of her orgasm. Also, the fear of losing emotional or physical control can also prevent a woman from relaxing and allowing the orgasm to happen.

Anger, resentment, and a lack of trust with a partner are some of the biggest inhibitors of female orgasm. A woman must feel safe, secure, and desired to allow her orgasmic potential to be realized.

COITAL PAIN

Vaginismus is the recurrent and persistent spasm of the musculature of outer muscles of the vagina. It prohibits physical intercourse because of the pain experienced and, in many cases, the physical impossibility of penetration. It is important to treat vaginismus as quickly as possible to prevent a conditioned response which will only be harder to treat effectively. Vaginismus is psychological in origin. There are personality and family of origin beliefs and attitudes that appear to contribute to this disorder.

Functional Dyspareunia refers to male-female intercourse associated with recurrent or persistent pain, in either the male or the female. Arousal difficulties, vaginismus, and medical problems must be ruled out before this can be accurately diagnosed. As with many of the sexual dysfunctions, psychosocial factors, rigid and strict upbringing, shame issues, and history of sexual abuse appear to be the major etiological factors with nonmedical dyspareunia.

FREQUENCY DISSATISFACTION

Many couples seek counseling because of differences in desire for sexual play. These differences may indicate deeper sexual or emotional issues. These can often be resolved by seeing a competent sex therapist.

TIME TO SEE A PROFESSIONAL?

If you tried some of the practices in this playbook and have been discouraged by the lack of participation either by you or your partner, it is time to consult a professional.

If you think you or your partner suffer from one or more of the dysfunctions described in this Appendix, it is time to see a professional. A competent marriage counselor will assist you in getting medical care if indicated. Sexual problems always include psychological components.

Look for a counselor experienced with couples and sexuality. Avoid exclusive individual therapy; it may not be good for relationship. If you wish to do individual psychotherapy and there are significant relationship issues, a combination of individual and couple work may be the most useful. Even if you have tried counseling before, try it again with a new counselor. It's important to get a good "fit." Look for a therapist who is direct about his/her work with sexual issues. Research has shown that the two biggest reasons counseling isn't helpful for a couple are: 1) the couple waits too long before seeing a therapist, or 2) they don't stay in therapy long enough. Take action now.

Safer Sex, Smart Sex

Although this book is written for the monogamous, heterosexual couple, we believe it important to mention safer sex. If either partner has any concerns about contracting any kind of infection (even a cold), or getting pregnant, there will be a part of that person that isn't totally present for any loving experience you may be having.

Fear of pregnancy can rob you of pleasurable sexual experiences. This could happen if a woman is changing forms of birth control or is using a method of birth control that isn't as reliable as others. In this case, the male would be wise to use a condom until both felt confident with the new method of birth control. It's very important to communicate to your partner any information that might help him/her feel comfortable and safe.

If one partner has Herpes, special care must be taken to protect your partner during an outbreak. An exposed male would be wise to use a condom several days after the site appears to have dried up. If the female partner has active lesions, be very careful around the affected area and use a lubricant with Nonoxynol 9 as well as rubber gloves and condoms.

During and after anal play, be sure no fecal matter or anal juices come in contact with the vaginal area. A serious vaginal infection can result. Men, be sure to urinate right after anal sex to prevent urethral infection or use a condom. Of course, thorough washing with warm soap and water is necessary as well.

If in doubt about the chances of pregnancy or spreading a virus or bacterial infection, the safest protection is a condom or surgical latex gloves with a layer of lubricant containing Nonoxynol 9 on the penis or hand, followed by a coating on the outside of the condom or latex glove. Nonoxynol 9 has been found to effectively lessen the risk of many infections including the AIDS virus. Many women and men find Nonoxynol 9 irritating. Be aware.

SAFER SEX

You may want to experiment with another barrier method of protection while engaging in oral-genital sex or kissing. It can be fun to try for variety and the experience. This involves the use of a plastic wrap such as Saran Wrap or Glad Wrap. Use a piece large enough to cover the area around both mouths or the mouth and genitals of either sex. Hint: This little trick can prevent one of the most contagious of socially transmitted diseases, the common cold.

The safest sex with an infected partner is abstinence. If you choose to be sexual anyway—be as safe as you can be. Be responsible.

Information for Therapists Using This Playbook

This playbook has been written with the explicit purpose of using it in conjunction with marriage or relationship counseling/therapy. Not only is it packed with information that the therapist might find useful, there are many practices that can enhance the therapist's efforts to assist the clients.

The chapters can be offered to the clients as homework, either in part or whole. With a couple who is resistant to homework or insecure about doing practices on his/her own, the therapist can introduce the practice in the context of the session. In other words, use a practice as a demonstration or experience. You, the therapist, will learn more valuable information about the dynamics of the relationship.

We do not recommend that this playbook just be handed to a couple. It is not an all-purpose, fix-the-relationship manual. It has been designed for the committed couple who wants their relationship to be even better, now and in the future.

The pronouns in the book have been used to avoid discrimination against gay and lesbian couples. This book can easily be used with alternative lifestyle couples of any orientation.

We, the authors, very much want this playbook to be user-friendly for both the therapist and the couple. Should you desire a telephone or e-mail consultation with Dr. TallTrees or Orv. Fry, MFT, please send an e-mail.

E-mail Dr. TallTrees at Jeffre@TantraAtTahoe.com or e-mail Mr. Fry at Orv@Ignitersoftheheart.com.

Index

acceptance, 12, 193
  of others, 14
  self-, 12, 193
acknowledgments, 52, 98
actions, responsibility for, 93
affection, 6, 89, 97, 98, 120
affirmation, 74, 75, 76, 77, 91
anal sex, 141
anger, 21, 88, 91, 92, 93, 102, 107, 117, 192
  origins of, 88
  owning your, 89
  time out, 92
attitudes, 11, 14, 15, 17, 85, 138, 162, 174, 193
  differences, 129
  inappropriate, 13
  new, 148
  non-judgmental, 11, 14

balance, 66, 71, 191
blaming, 21
body image, 72, 74, 78

cleanliness, 112
co-creation, 43, 47
commitment, 43, 47, 70
  lack of, 15

communication, 5, 11, 20, 189
  intimate, 20, 26
  meta-, 31
  nurturing, 31
  quality of, 20
compliments, 52, 53, 190
conflict, 22, 40, 82, 90, 165, 202
  ripe for, 70
  to avoid, 22
courage, 45–46, 48, 194
criticism, 18, 24, 42, 52, 149, 157
culture, sex-positive, 82
cunnilingus, 10, 138, 143, 150

dancing, 176
date night, 161
decompression time, 70
dildoes, 177
double standards, 85

ecstasy, 6, 46, 48, 183, 187, 188
emotional
  intimacy, 81
  safety, 48
erections, 115
eroticism, 3, 154

fantasy, 58, 132, 153, 155, 157, 159, 163

fear, 13, 15, 23, 37, 47, 95, 194, 212
  of receiving, 166
  of rejection, 44
  of unknown, 18
feelings, responsibility for, 93
fellatio, 138
female G spot, 140
flirting, 105, 106, 109
foreplay, 109, 124, 162
freedom, 47

gender differences, 21, 81, 121, 138
guilt, 6, 23, 117, 128, 131, 163, 188

health, 70
healthy sexual person, 187
heart, 48, 77, 101, 142, 185
honesty, 18, 32, 38, 44, 174

infatuation, 96
inhibited sexual drive, 117
integrity, 45, 46
intercourse, 4, 115, 124, 149, 165, 177, 194
  anal, 140
intimacy, xi, xii, xiv, 22, 189

215

intimacy *(continued)*
  emotional, 43, 81, 100
  myth of, 30
  preventing, 87

listening, 12, 14, 29, 189
  guidelines for, 29
love, xii, 44, 46, 96
  giving and receiving, 99
loveplay, 109, 124, 153

male G spot, 139
masturbation, 128, 149, 157
mind reading, 21

oral sex, 10, 137, 138, 139, 149

parents, critical, 11
passion, 57, 150, 154
  creating, 60
  elements of, 58
peaking, 135, 169
personal growth, 41, 183
  discourage, 15
  promote, 14
positive stroking, 52
powerless, 90
powerlessness, 24, 38, 40, 88, 91
present time, 114
priority,
  relationship, 191
  sexuality, 191

prostate, 139

relationship, 32, 35, 53, 66, 75, 97, 120, 155, 163
  celebrating the, 195
  loving, 18
  rescue in, 36, 40
  ripple, 43
relaxing, 118
rescuing, 36, 48
resentment, 33, 88, 91, 192
respect, 33, 188
risking, 190, 194
romance, 101, 103, 176, 192, 196

self-acceptance, 12, 193
self-esteem, 75
  high, 45
self, honoring, 192
self-image, 72, 75
self-pleasuring, 128, 129, 130, 159
self-validation, 22
setting the mood, 108
sex, xii, 3–5
  adventurous, 175
  ecstatic, 184
  education, 5
  healthy, 5
  playful, 5
  -positive person, 149
  red hot, 48
  toys, 177

sexual,
  agendas, 107
  beliefs, 5
  boredom, xii
  desire, 57, 74, 121
  enhancers, 176
sexuality, 3, 4, 6
  human, 142
  women, 116
shame, 6, 117, 128, 166, 185, 210
spirituality, 181, 195
stroke, 53, 55, 190
  receiving a, 53
stroking, emotional, 54
support, 33, 35, 190, 196
  authentic, 40, 41
  emotional, 46, 51
  lack of, 149

testosterone, 162
time,
  decompression, 70
  demands for, 66
trust, 23, 44–45, 48, 190
truth, xi, 23, 25, 31, 40, 44, 190, 192,

vibrators, 177
victimized, 36
vulnerability, 44, 46, 70, 183

withholds, 192

About the Authors

Jeffre TallTrees, Ph.D., is a licensed psychologist and sex therapist who has been working with couples and singles in private practice in Northern California since 1979. She is wholistic and pragmatic in her clinical work. She has written a weekly newspaper column for over thirteen years. Dr. TallTrees currently resides in North Lake Tahoe with her beloved husband and their two Golden Retrievers. She is an avid downhill and cross-country skier and mountain biker, and enjoys hiking and camping.

Orv Fry, MA, MFT, holds a Master's Degree in Marriage and Family therapy and has been specializing in relationship and sexuality counseling for over twenty-eight years. Orv worked in private practice with Dr. Jeffre TallTrees at Danville Psychology Associates in Danville, California for thirteen years. Orv is a frequent lecturer and presenter at conferences and symposiums on relationship and sexuality. He helped to create the intern program for the Human Awareness Institute. Together with his wife, Maeve Udell Fry, Orv coaches and inspires individuals, couples, and groups to have more fulfilling and dynamic relationships and lives. Orv and Maeve live in Grass Valley, California, where Orv was born and raised. He is a passionate water skier and barefoot skier.

Printed in the United Kingdom
by Lightning Source UK Ltd.
9371300001B